MILNER CRAFT SERIES

IMAGINATIVE BRUSHWORK

MILNER CRAFT SERIES

IMAGINATIVE BRUSHWORK

MEROPE MILLS

PHOTOGRAPHY BY RODNEY WEIDLAND

SALLY MILNER PUBLISHING

First published in 1992 by
Sally Milner Publishing Pty Ltd
558 Darling Street
Rozelle NSW 2039 Australia

Reprinted 1994

Design by Wing Ping Tong
Photography by Rodney Weidland
Typeset in Australia by Asset Typesetting Pty Ltd
Printed in Australia by Impact Printing

National Library of Australia
Cataloguing-in-Publication data:

Mills, Merope.
Imaginative brushwork.

ISBN 1 86351 089 3.

1. Painting — Technique. 2. Decorative arts — Technique.
3. Folk art. I. Title. (Series : Milner craft series).

745.723

This book is dedicated to Neville
for his enthusiasm and encouragement

ACKNOWLEDGEMENTS

I would like to thank the following people for their assistance:

Norma Reimann and Charmaine de Freistos for sharing their wonderful talent with me.

My mother for the exquisite embroidery.

Robert and Sarah Hayse Gregson of The Mosman Clock shop for their help and support.

Christopher Hall for the beautifully turned needlecases.

Susie Strudwick and her father for supplying me with Swiss boxes over the years.

Rodney Weidland for his exceptional photography.

Sally Milner.

Diana Challinor.

Foreword

Once or twice in a lifetime there crosses one's path an exceptional treasure. So it is for me in my friendship with Merope Mills, and so it is for those who have had the pleasure to acquire one of her precious works of art. Merope's talents lie not only in her skills in imaginative brushwork but also in her gifts of giving and sharing with others. This book has been written for those who enjoy the same love of nature, friendship, home and creativity. Her 'heirlooms of tomorrow' are made up of the memories of her past and represent the very essence of the artist herself.

Merope's technical training as a layout artist and later as a teacher, graduating with distinction, has provided her with the structure and confidence needed in her vocation today, but it is the nostalgia for her loving home in South Africa, where she first learnt painting with Norma Reimann, and her years in Kent with her husband, Neville, that have influenced her work the most.

Their home today in Mosman is adorned with the cherished reminders of the people and places she loves. An artistic family inspires much of her creativity; her sister Marianthe paints beautiful watercolour studies of flowers and these grace the walls of Merope's home and are echoed in her glorious garden, while the intricate designs and rich textures of her mother's embroidery can be seen around the house in scatter cushions, tablecloths and hand-stitched rugs. (These have also been used to complement much of the photographic work in the book.) A treasured friendship quilt is testament to the bonding and loyalty of close companions.

The love of art, patchwork and quiltmaking has sealed the friendship of our own little mutual admiration group first established in Merope's earliest folk art classes in 1982. We meet regularly with Merope to inspire and encourage each other in our ever-challenging need to create and develop new designs and artistic endeavours, and for many years we held a very successful annual fair.

Merope's personal interest and flair for interior decoration is recognised in the fact that all three of the homes she and Neville have lived in since moving to Sydney have featured in national magazines and all reflect her love of hearth and home. Her years in the UK have shaped the direction in which her designs now travel. The English countryside, with its thatched cottages and abundant spring gardens are the focal point of her work today. Thus romanticised pastoral imagery marries well with Merope's inventive use of découpage, which she studied in South Africa.

Ever respectful of the traditions of European Baüernmalerei and American Folk Art, Merope is, however, never confined by convention; her imagination is always open to and receptive of new interpretations and altering perspectives in decorative art.

After six years of concentrated work for exhibitions and private commissions Merope has now returned to teaching her craft, focusing on a more personalised expression of folk art. Cottages and country gardens, découpage and intricate lacework, miniatures and pastel shades have replaced the more stylised forms and darker tones of traditional Baüernmalerei. Her extensive collection of old world verses adds the final touch to her truly unique and imaginative brushwork. Merope now conducts workshops throughout New South Wales, interstate and in New Zealand. Many of her former students are experienced artists and teachers themselves and acknowledge the considerable influence she has had on their work.

This book represents just a small collection of the jewels of her creation; they are indeed treasures to be collected and held for posterity.

Congratulations Merope, your book is an inspiration and delight to all who read it.

DIANA CHALLINOR

Contents

Requirements and Methods

Sandpaper

I find medium sandpaper is the best. Use a wooden block to ensure even pressure and always sand along the grain before you base coat the article. I use WET AND DRY black sandpaper as well.

Base Coat

I use Jo Sonja's paint for my backgrounds. It is good quality and one can mix any colour and shade. If you are painting a large piece of furniture it would be advisable to look into acrylic or water based paint that is sold in a larger quantity.

Always give your piece two coats of paint, sanding in between coats.

A large flat 1″ brush, e.g. SILVERADO SERIES 1151 ART BASICS JAPAN is suitable for painting the background.

Make sure your strokes all go the same way to ensure smooth painting without any ridges.

Stylus and Graphite Paper

You will need a stylus and graphite paper for transferring the design onto the wooden piece. Have a light colour (yellow or white) for dark backgrounds and a dark colour (blue or charcoal or black) for light backgrounds.

Cut the tracing out to the size of the wooden piece, secure it with masking tape on top and slide the graphite paper under it. You are then ready to trace the design with a round tipped stylus, which is available from art suppliers, or you can use an empty ballpoint pen to equal effect.

Paint Brushes

For the main work I use only RAPHAEL (S)8404 MATRE KOLINSKY FRANCE round brushes, Numbers 0, 1, 2, 3 and 5.

If you are a beginner invest in a No. 2 brush as it is suitable for just about all the painting. These are all sable brushes.

For borders I use a flat brush: e.g. ⅛″ and ¼″ PROLENE by PRO ARTE 106 ENGLAND.

You will need a stipple brush as well. I just use old brushes cut square.

Palette

I use plastic wrap that has been stretched over a China dinner plate. The wrap can be easily discarded after use.

Paper Towelling

Two sheets of paper towelling next to your palette is necessary so as to absorb excess water from your paint brush.

Paints

I use JO SONJA'S ARTISTS colours and MATISSE PROFESSIONAL ARTISTS ACRYLIC colour. If MATISSE is not available I have given alternatives.

Sealer

I use JO SONJA'S ALL-PURPOSE SEALER or MATISSE SEALER.

Patina (Antiquing)

Patina means to age a piece of work. It mellows the colours and softens the end result.

You will need:
Clean fluff-free cloths or rags
FEAST WATSON — CLEAR SCANDINAVIAN OIL (MATT DANISH OIL FINISH) or other matt oil
WINDSOR AND NEWTON BURNT UMBER artists' oil paint

METHOD

Dampen a clean cloth or rag with the Scandinavian oil, then squeeze out a little Burnt Umber onto the middle of your painted piece. With the dampened cloth rub the oil paint all over your work, adding more oil on your cloth if necessary. Don't worry if it is too dark or too light because at this stage (as it is still wet) you can control the colour.

If you want to lighten the work, take a clean cloth and rub off some of the oil paint. You can add more Scandinavian oil to your cloth and wipe even more paint off.

If you want to darken your work simply add more Burnt Umber and rub all over.

For tricky corners and borders use an old paint brush dipped in the oil, then wipe smooth with a cloth.

Make sure you are satisfied with the colour. Once it is dry it cannot be lightened again. However, you can add more Burnt Umber and oil and darken it again.

Rub all excess Scandinavian oil well into the piece. Leave it for a minimum of a day and night before varnishing. Make sure it is dry before you varnish. If it is not dry it will go streaky as you apply the varnish.

VARNISHING

You will need:
Brush: Flat 1″ brush
Varnish: FEAST WATSON — SATINPROOF (an oil-based polyurethane varnish) or other satin finish varnish

METHOD

Paint the varnish over all the work using even brush strokes going in one direction only. Make sure there are no runs around corners and borders.

After the first coat is dry (at least 24 hours) sand very lightly with BLACK WET AND DRY SANDPAPER. You do not use water with the sandpaper. Wipe the powdery excess with a 'tack cloth' and give the work a second coat. Let it dry thoroughly and sand again, a little more vigorously now. Wipe with a tack cloth and give the work a third and final coat.

The varnishing brush can be left in a jar filled with turpentine for the length of time of applying the varnish (4–5 days). But every time you finish varnishing, clean all excess varnish by first dipping the brush into the turps and then onto absorbent paper, so ridding the brush of as much varnish as possible. Then leave it in the jar making sure the hair of the brush is well covered.

If the brush is not being used for a long period, clean the brush with turps and absorbent paper. Then wash it thoroughly with very hot water and dishwashing liquid. Rinse thoroughly in hot water and let it dry. It must have no trace of moisture when you want to use it again. If there is any water present, your painting will bubble up when you apply the varnish.

For antiquing and varnishing I use surgical gloves, as the stain and varnish are difficult to get off your hands.

Basic Techniques

I use paint of various consistency. Thin, flowing or watery paint, I mix with water until it pours like milk. Thickly mixed paint is the consistency of a very rich cream. Otherwise, I use the paint dry.

Comma Painting

To start off you will need to be able to handle your paint brush and control your paint.

The 'comma stroke' forms the basis of Folk Art.

You hold the brush exactly as you would when writing with a pencil or pen.

Fill the brush with paint, keeping the metal ferrule clean. Turn or swirl the brush in the paint so that it comes to a point, then pick up a drop of paint on the tip of the brush.

With one smooth stroke of the brush you paint commas, placing it down and then lifting slowly up, with no jerks. They can go straight down or to the left or to the right (Fig. 1).

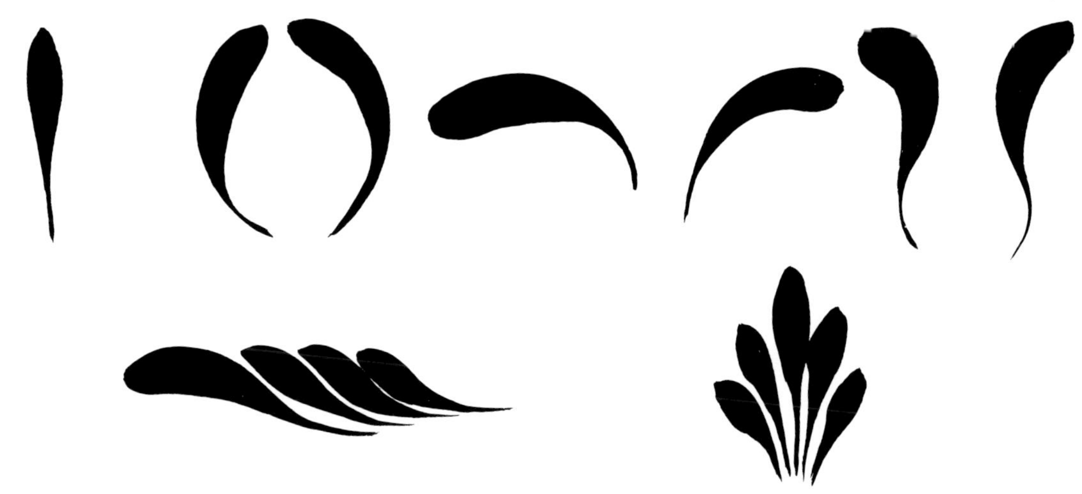

1

Variations on Commas

Load your brush but do not pick up a drop of paint on the tip of your brush. Start with the point of brush and use only light pressure, then heavy pressure for the middle, then lift up, so ending with a pointed tail (Fig. 2).

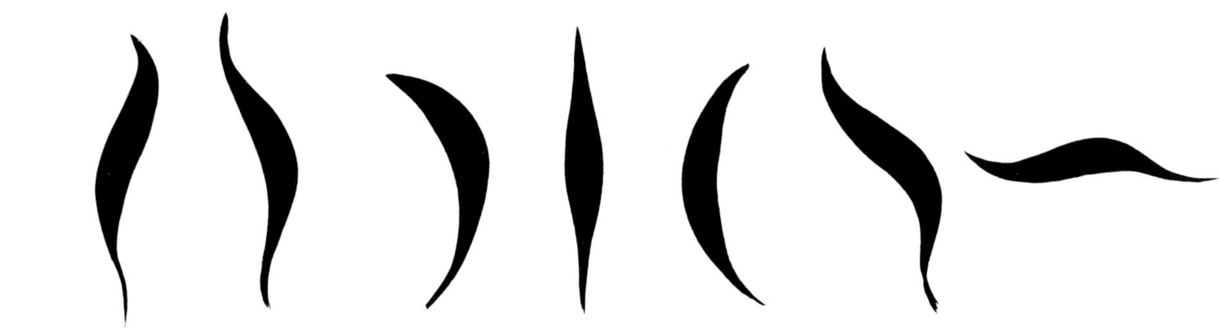

2

Dots

To paint dots (Fig. 3) load your brush with a drop of paint on the tip. Hold the brush straight up and drop the drop of paint down. As you lighten the pressure the dots will get smaller.

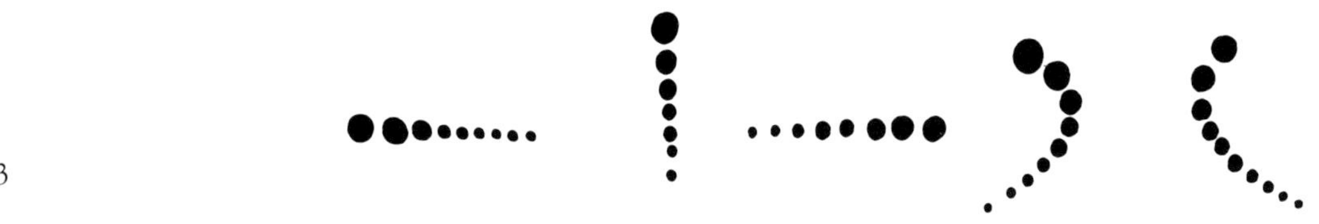

3

Lines

To paint fine lines add a little more water to the paint so that it will flow more readily. Swirl or turn the brush in the paint to form a perfect point, then holding the brush straight up paint a line with the tip of your brush. If the paint is too watery the line will be thick instead of fine.

The same method is used for outlining, veins of leaves and lettering.

Dry Brush Work

I use this method in many pieces of my work to (a) add texture and (b) for shading or highlighting.

Press out colours required onto your palette and allow to stand a while to thicken. Clean your brush and then wipe dry on absorbent paper, getting rid of all water. Do not add any water to the paint.

Flatten the brush in paint and wipe the flattened brush on paper towel. Make sure the hairs are fanned out. Lightly skim over work with just the tips of the brush. Build the intensity of colour up gradually with a few coats of paint.

Wet Brush Work

Wet Brush Work is used for shading. Unlike the previous method you use a wet brush on a wet background. For example, I will describe how I paint a rose (as in Needlecase page 41 and Patchwork Box page 58):

METHOD

- Paint base colour of Rose (Fig. 4).
- In a darker shade paint the centre, the bowl of the rose and the shading in the petals.
- With a clean brush blend the two colours just where they meet.

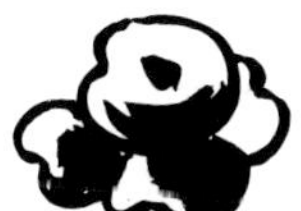

4

Sideloading

Sideloading is the term used for picking up two separate colours of paint.

METHOD

- Load the brush in one colour.
- Pick up a second colour on the side of your brush. You can direct this highlight or sideload to where you want it — to the top, or to the left or right, depending on where you need the highlight.

Daisies

Daisies are wonderful fillers and I use them in most of my work, to lighten and soften the design (Fig. 5).

METHOD

- Roll brush in paint, so forming a point.
- Pick up a drop of paint and paint a comma.
- Repeat four or more times, fanning out and forming a circle.
- Paint a dot in the middle.

These are the main brushstrokes and techniques I use. As you experiment you will no doubt add to these to create your own effects.

5

Sewing Box

Work, work, work
Seam, and gusset, and band,
Band, and gusset, and seam,
Till over the buttons I fall asleep
And sew them on in a dream!

Thomas Hood: *The Song of the Shirt*

Requirements:
You will need a round box measuring 31 cm (12¼ inches) in diameter, plus small boxes that fit into the large box.
Brushes: Raphael No. 1, 2 and 3
Stipple Brush

Palette: Jo Sonja's — Smoked Pearl
Teal Green
French Blue
Warm White
Provincial Beige
Carbon Black
Napthol Crimson
Yellow Oxide
Raw Umber
Red Earth
Green Oxide

Matisse — Antique Green or Jo Sonja's Teal Green with Fawn (mixed 1:1)

PREPARATION
Sand the boxes. Give them a wash of watery Smoked Pearl.
Sand again.

METHOD FOR MAIN BOX

- With a good compass draw in the four circles.
- Paint the circles in Teal Green.
- Trace the line of the wall and ground level.
- Paint the sky in a mixture of French Blue and Warm White.
- Stipple the tree in with Antique Green, then Teal Green, then Smoked Pearl using a stipple brush or an old brush cut square.
- The wall is painted in large stone blocks in shades of Smoked Pearl, and Provincial Beige mixed with Smoked Pearl and a touch of Carbon Black. Use paint thickly and apply with a dry brush.
- The lawn is painted in a mixture of Smoked Pearl plus Antique Green with a touch of Yellow Oxide.
- Lady (from a painting by Helen Allingham):

a. Trace lady, chicken coop and chickens.

b. Paint in lady as follows —
Hair: Provincial Beige
Dress: Smoked Pearl mixed with Provincial Beige
Skirt: French Blue
Basket: Provincial Beige
Shoes: Carbon Black
Skin: A mixture of Provincial Beige, Warm White and Napthol Crimson
Give a second coat to all these parts.

c. Shading
Hair: Using the Dry Brush Method shade hair and bun with Warm White mixed with Yellow Oxide. Add deeper shading in a mixture of Provincial Beige and Raw Umber.
Face and Hands: Shade with Warm White.
Dress: Use very thick Warm White for gathers and folds, ie: curve of the back, sleeves, gathers in the waist, the folds as the dress is pinned back.
Skirt: Highlight with French Blue mixed with Warm White. Paint the deep folds in French Blue mixed with Carbon Black.
Shoes: Black with Provincial Beige.
Basket: Shade with Raw Umber mixed with Carbon Black and Yellow Oxide mixed with Warm White.

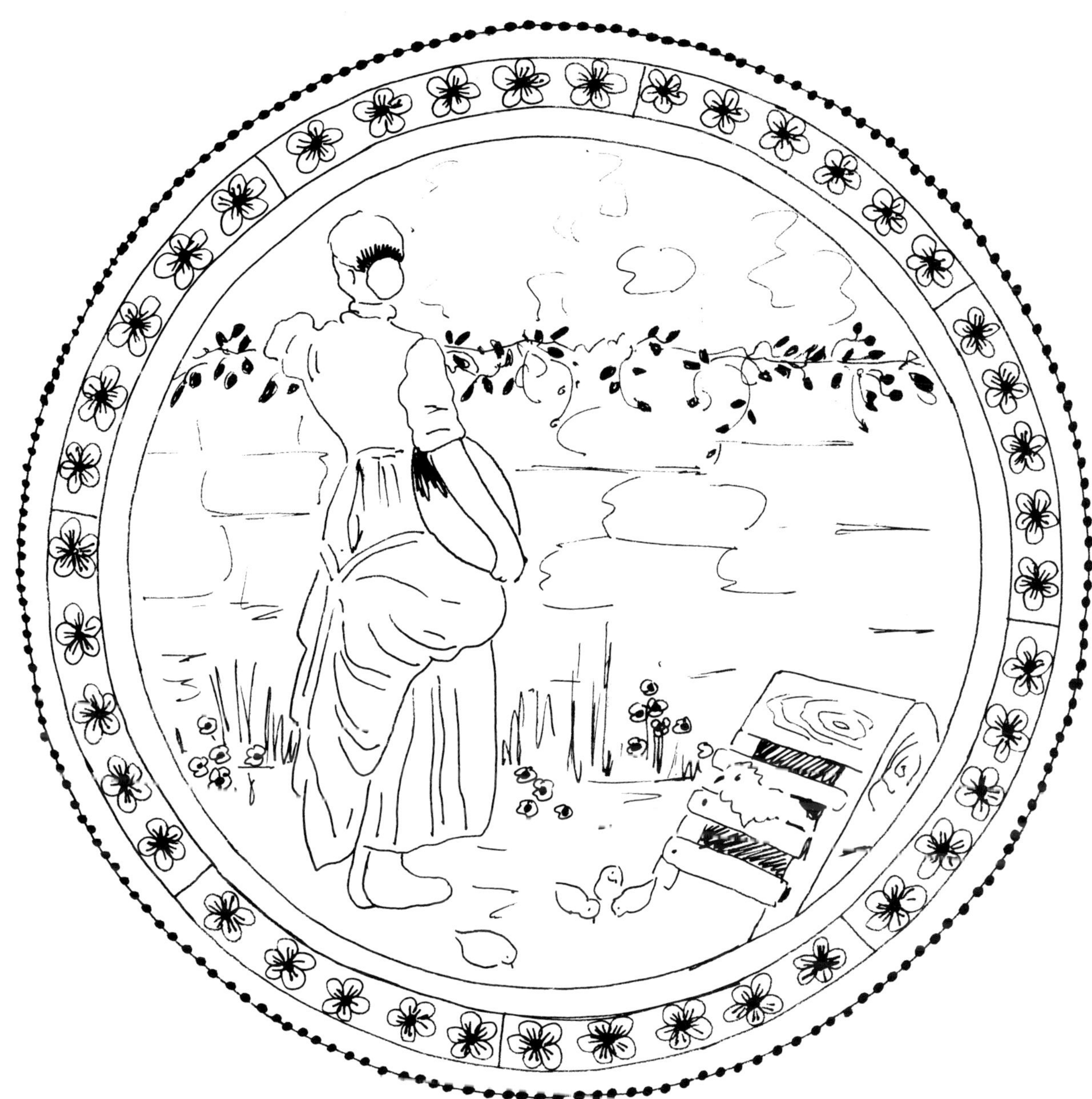

d. Chicken Coop
Paint coop in a mixture of Provincial Beige with Yellow Oxide and Warm White.
Inside the coop is Raw Umber with Carbon Black.
Paint the wood grain in Warm White with Yellow Oxide using the Dry Brush Method.

e. Hen
Paint the body with a mixture of Raw Umber and Yellow Oxide. The eye is White and the beak Black while the comb is Red Earth.

f. Chickens
Paint the body in Yellow Oxide with Warm White, and the eyes, beaks and feet in Carbon Black.

g. Ivy on the wall and leaves of daisies at the bottom of the wall should be painted a mixture of Teal Green and Black.

h. Daisies
These are Warm White with Red Earth centres.

i. Garland
The windflowers that form a garland around the lady are described in the Step-by-Step photographs and the instructions which follow.

j. Lines
Paint a fine line in French Blue around the edge of the lid on top. Paint a broader line in the same colour using ⅛″ flat brush and a thin line above it on the edge of the rim of the lid.
These lines are repeated on the smaller boxes.

k. Daisy border
The daisy border around the lady is done by alternating all the colours used on the lid, except for the Red Earth.

METHOD FOR SMALL BOXES

- Trace the oval design in the middle of the boxes.
- Paint the oval in French Blue.
- Paint the fine line just inside the oval in Warm White.
- Paint verses in Warm White.
- Paint leaves in Antique Green.
- Paint darker leaves in Teal Green.
- Paint daisies in Warm White.
- Paint Yellow Oxide centres to daisies.
- Antique.
- Varnish.

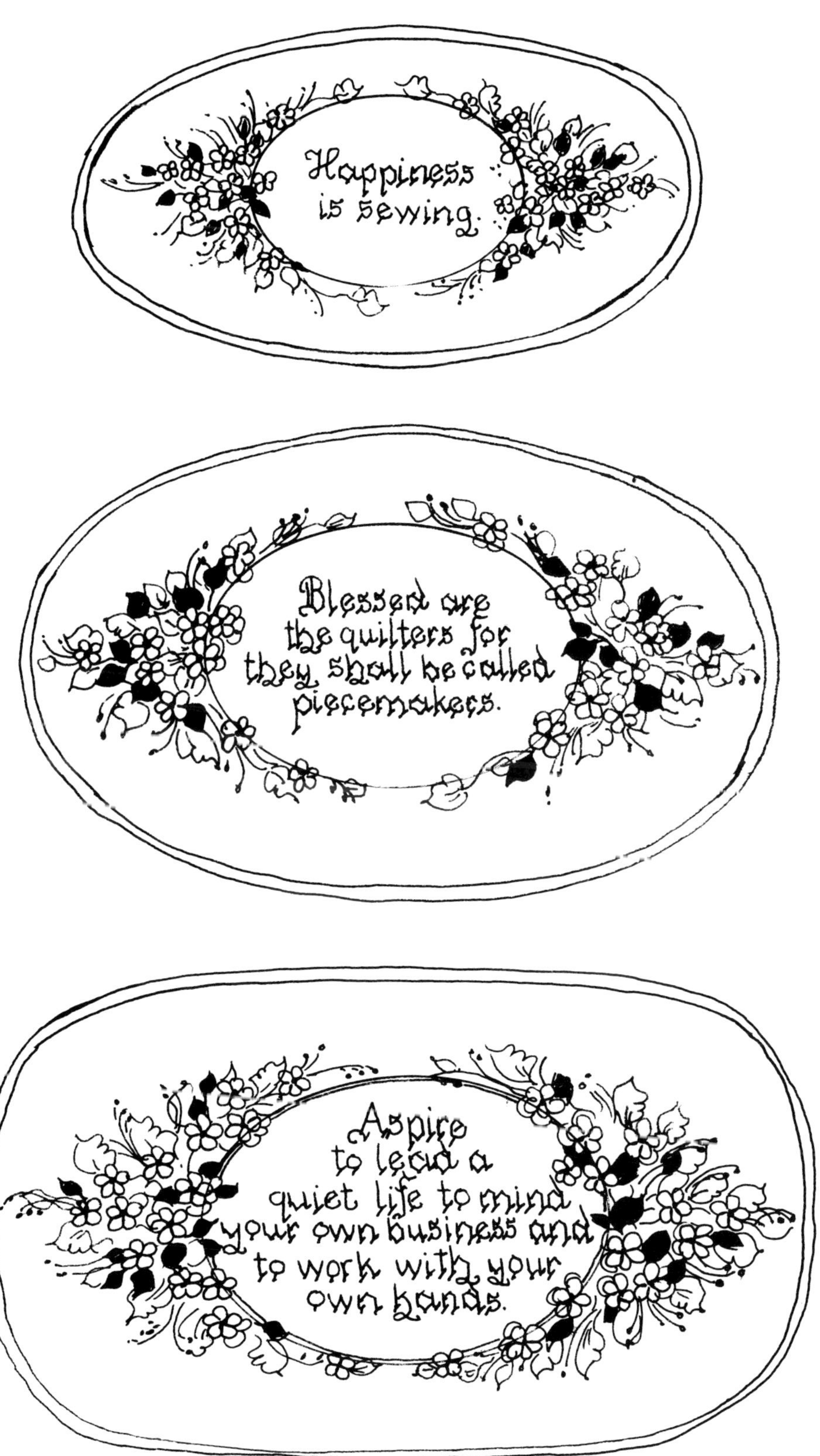
Happiness
is sewing.
Blessed are
the quilters for
they shall be called
piecemakers.
Aspire
to lead a
quiet life to mind
your own business and
to work with your
own hands.

Step-By-Step

GUIDE TO WINDFLOWERS

(See also colour section)

Step 1 Tracing of leaves
Trace the design of leaves onto the lid with blue graphite paper and a stylus.

Step 2 Painting leaves
Paint the leaves with watery Antique Green. Paint from the bottom of the leaf to the top (as if you were painting your nails) ending in a fine point at the tip of the leaf.

Step 3 Detail of leaves
Load your brush with a flowing Teal Green and roll it into a fine point. Using only the tip of your brush, outline the leaf on the one side and paint a squiggly line on the other side. Add two veins in the middle of the leaf.

Step 4 Tracing of flowers over leaves
Trace flowers and buds with blue graphite paper and a stylus.

Step 5 Base coat of flowers
Base coat flowers in Smoked Pearl. When dry give them a second coat.

Step 6 Shading of flowers
You might need to retrace the centre and overlapping petals of the flowers. Using the Wet Brush Method shade the centre with a watery Green Oxide and then with French Blue which surrounds the centre.

Step 7 Adding White to the petals
Using the Dry Brush Method pick up thick Warm White and pull the paint from the outer edge of the petal down towards the centre.

Step 8 Finishing Touches
Add Yellow Oxide dots around the centre. With a mixture of Teal Green and Carbon Black, paint in dark green leaves, commas, stems and calyxes as shown in the design.

Step 9 Antiqued and varnished completed work.

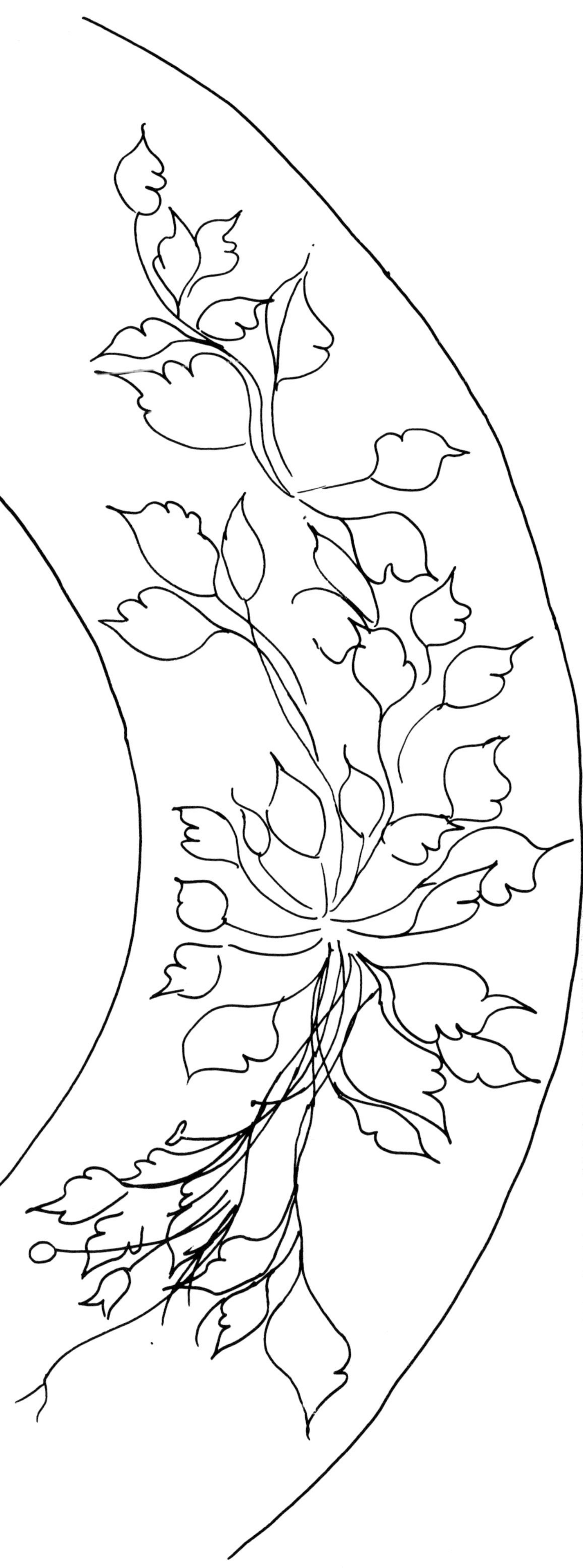

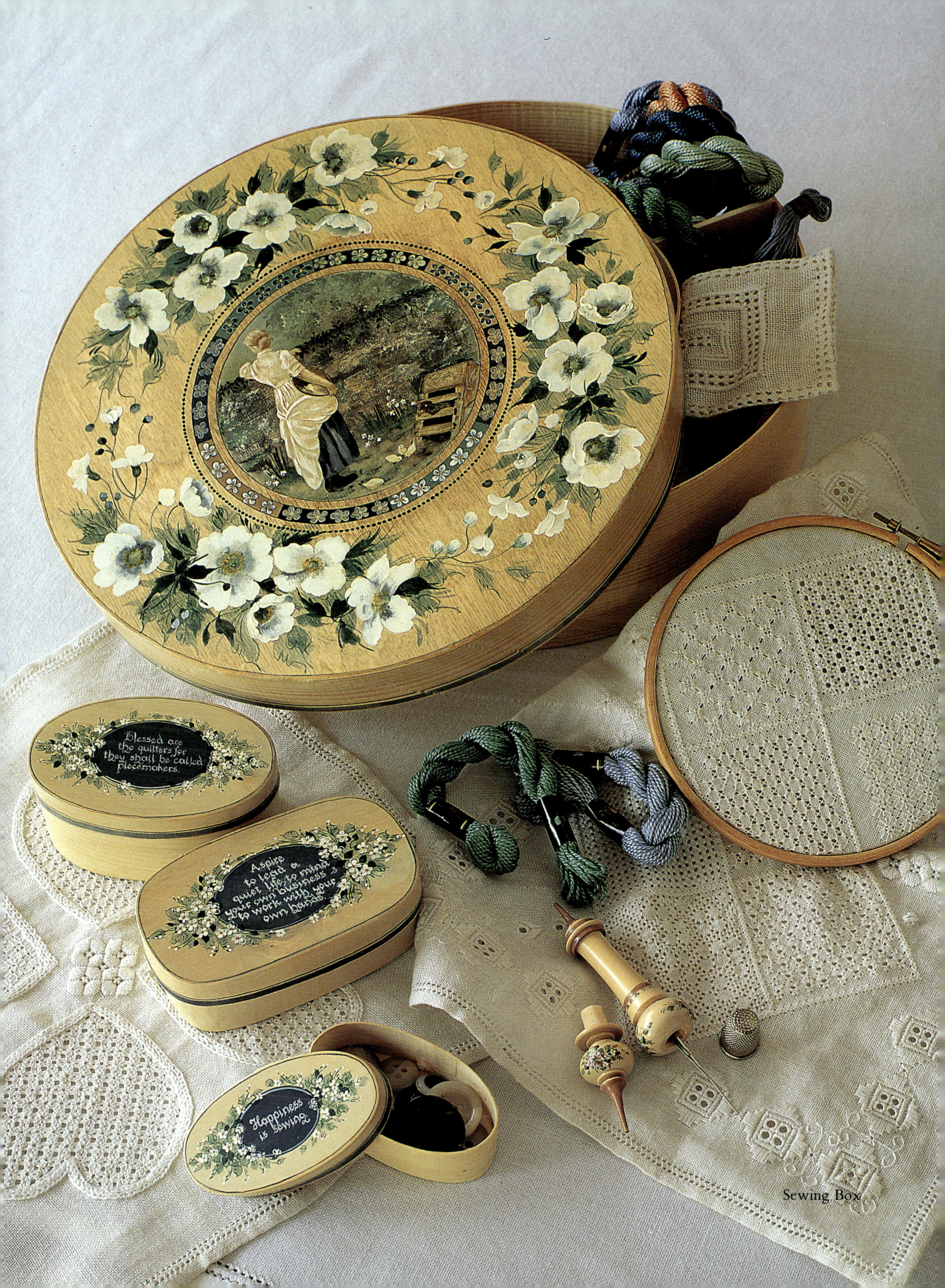
Blessed are the quilters for they shall be called piecemakers.
Aspire to lead a quiet life, to mind your own business & to work with your own hands.
Happiness is sewing

Sewing Box

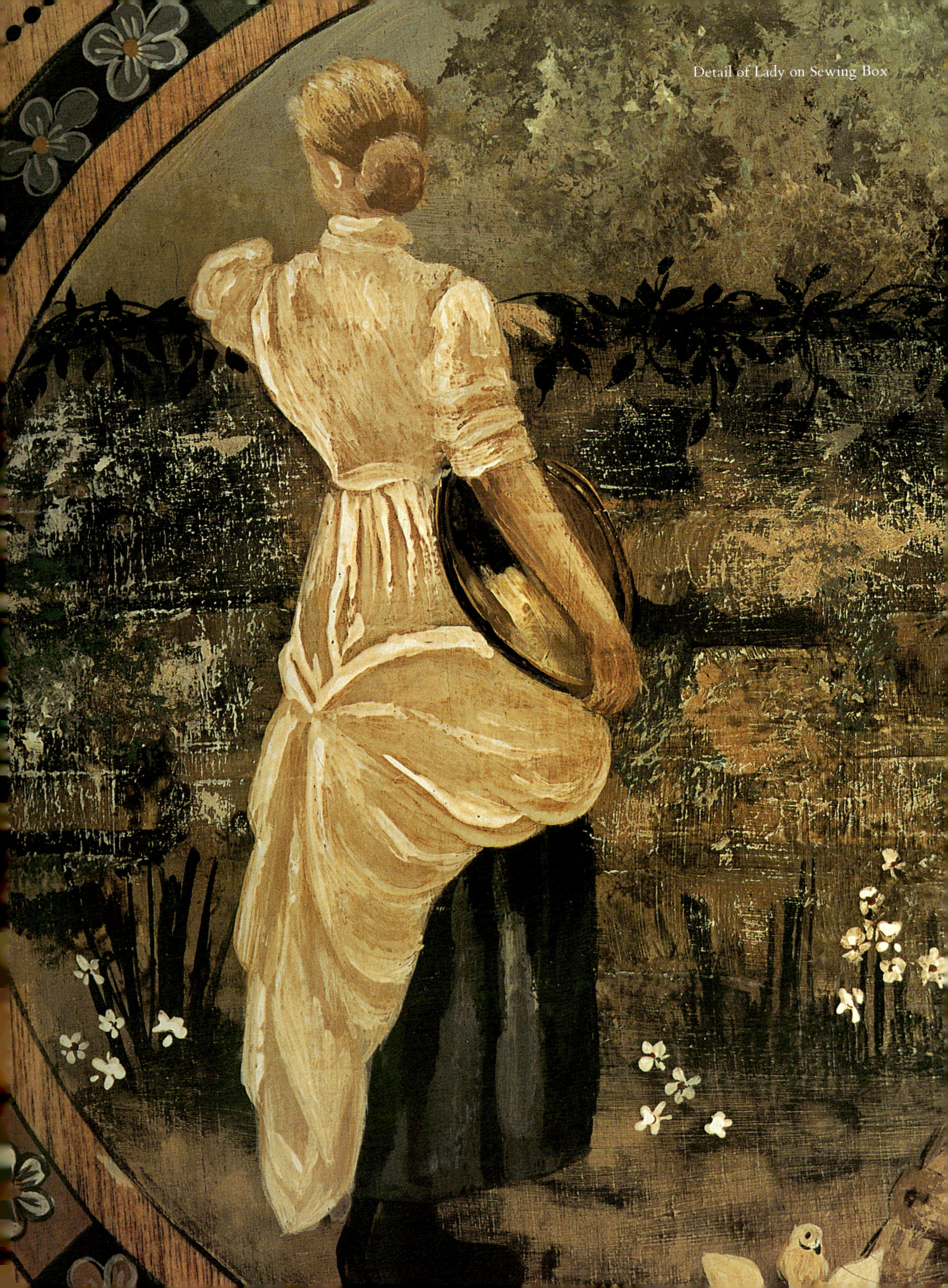

Detail of Lady on Sewing Box

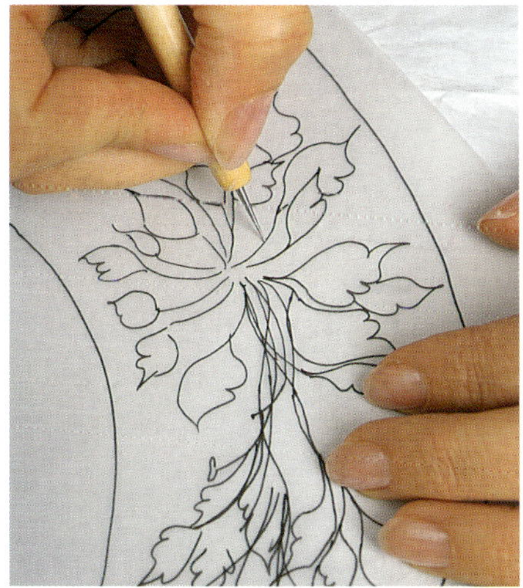

Step 1: Trace design of leaves onto lid with blue graphite paper and a stylus

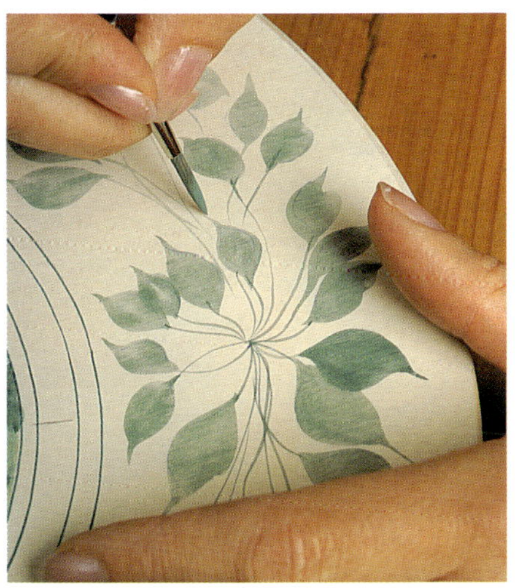

Step 2: Paint leaves with watery Antique Green. Paint from bottom of leaf to top (as if painting your nails), ending in a fine point at tip of leaf

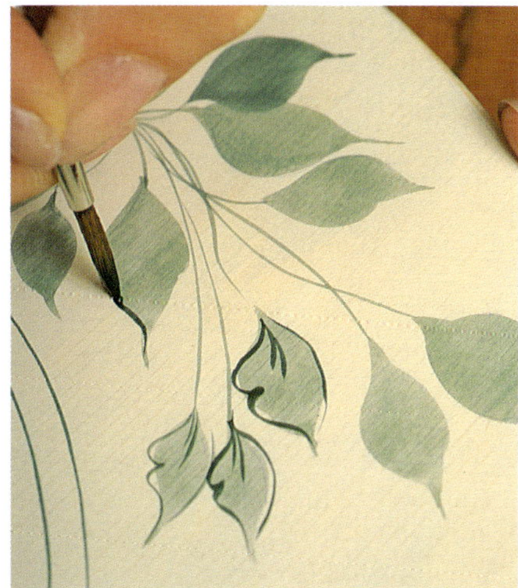

Step 3: Load brush with a flowing Teal Green and roll it into a fine point. Using only the tip of brush, outline leaf on one side and paint a squiggly line on other side. Add two veins in middle of leaf

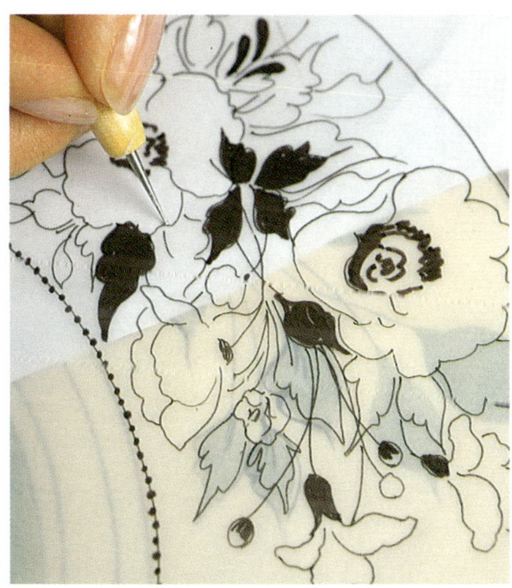

Step 4: Trace flowers and buds with blue graphite paper and a stylus

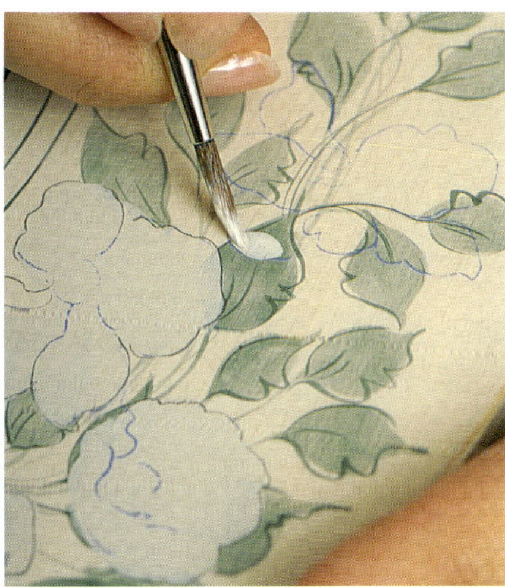

Step 5: Base coat flowers in Smoked Pearl. When dry give them a second coat

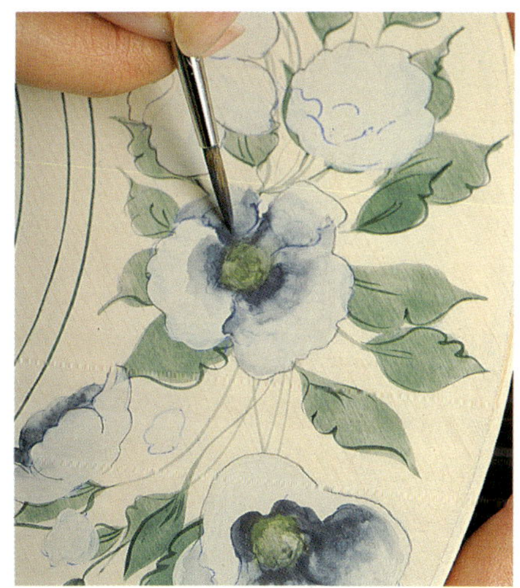

Step 6: You might need to retrace centre and overlapping petals of flowers. Using Wet Brush Method shade centre with a watery Green Oxide and then with French Blue which surrounds centre

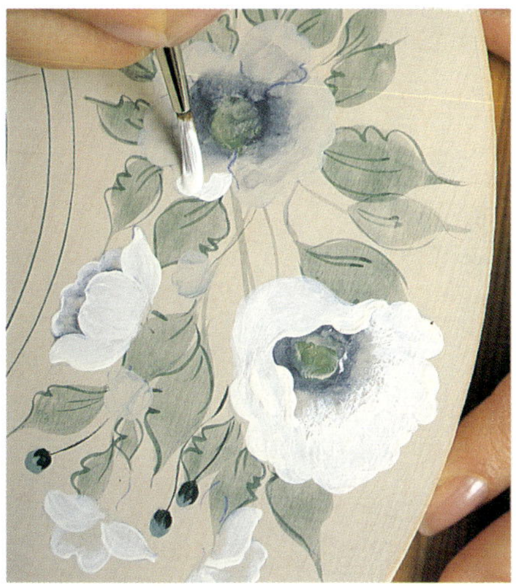

Step 7: Using Dry Brush Method pick up thick Warm White and pull paint from outer edge of petal down towards centre

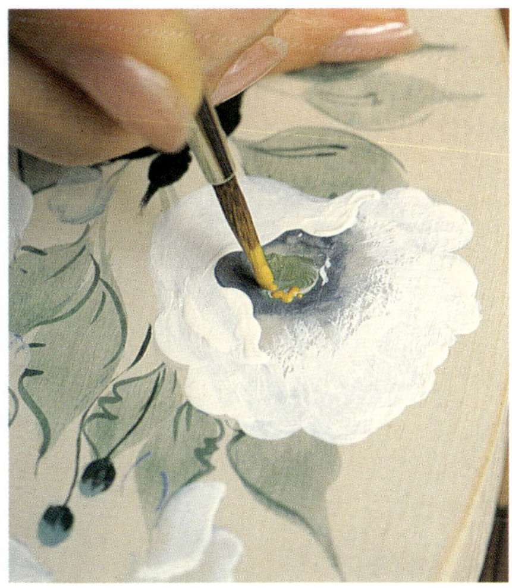

Step 8: Add Yellow Oxide dots around centre. With a mixture of Teal Green and Carbon Black, paint in dark green leaves, commas, stems and calyxes as shown in design

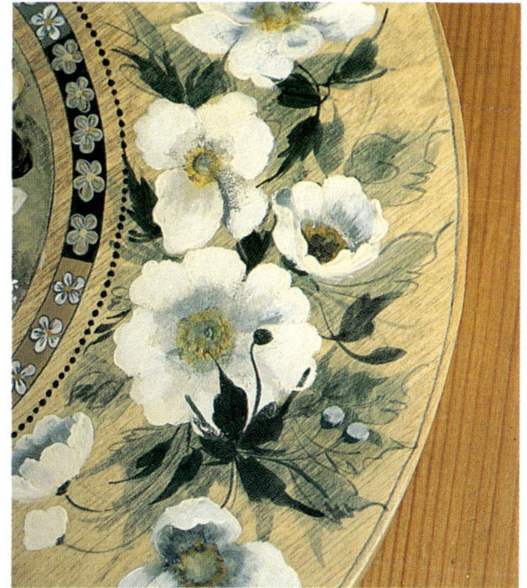

Step 9: Antiqued and varnished completed work

Antique Post Card Box

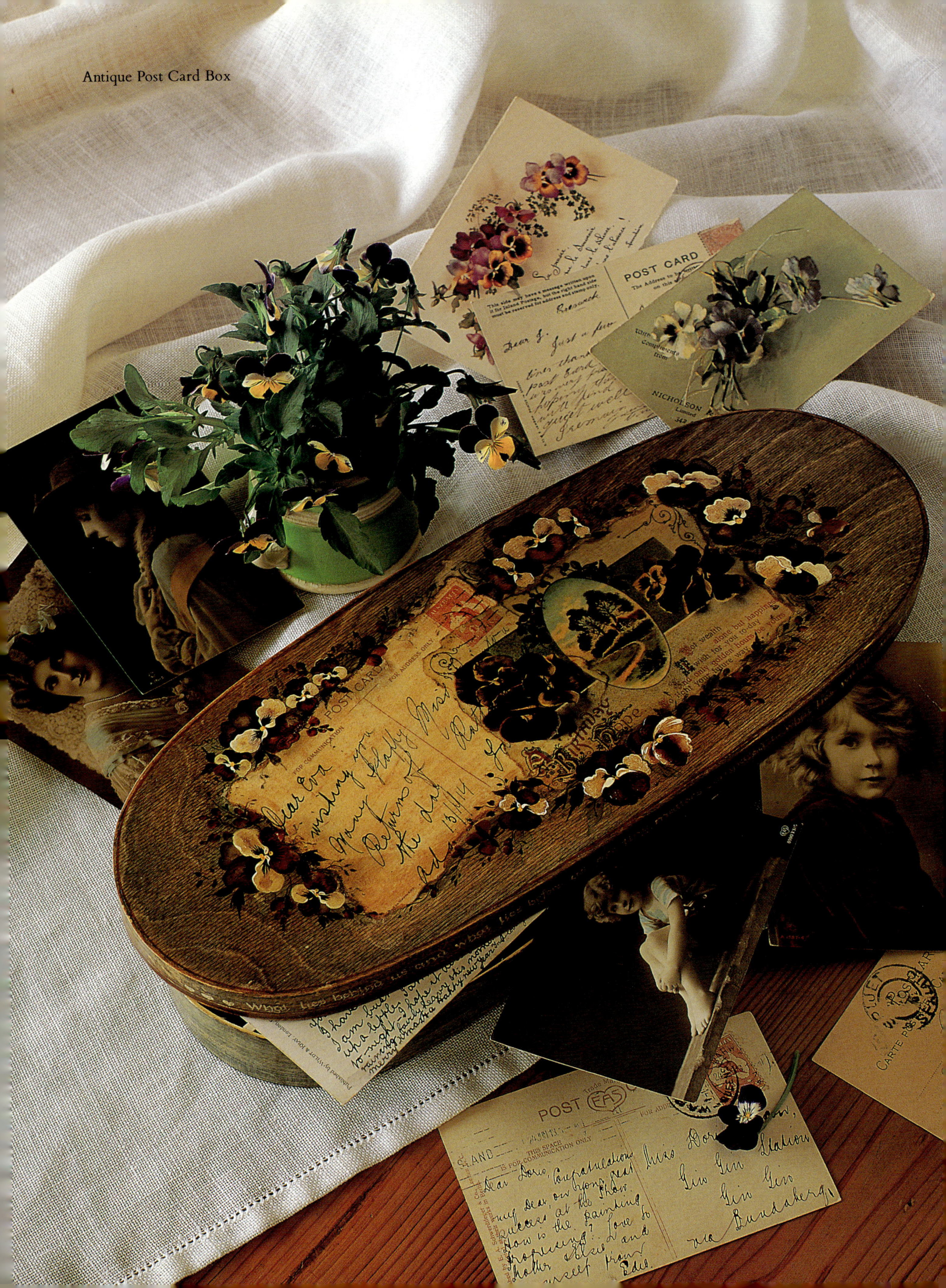

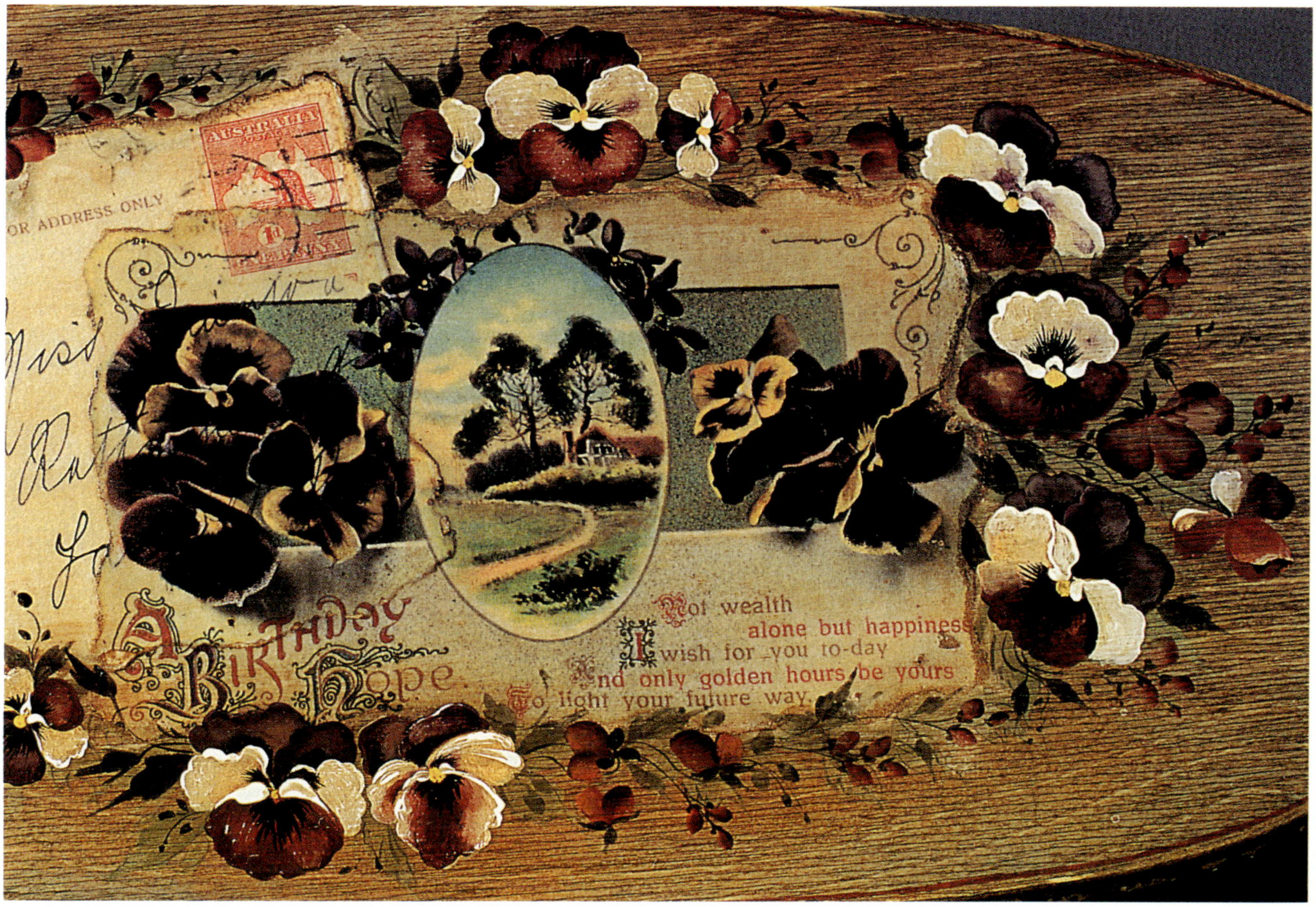

Detail of Pansies on Post Card Box

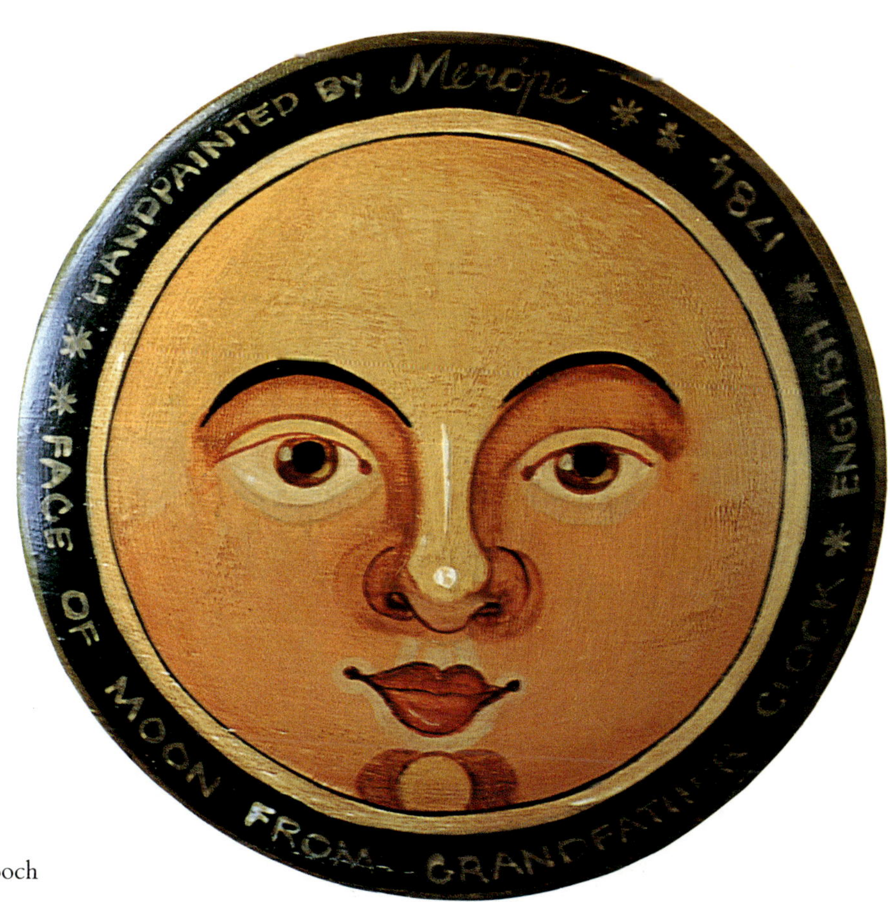

Detail of Moon Brooch

Moon Brooches

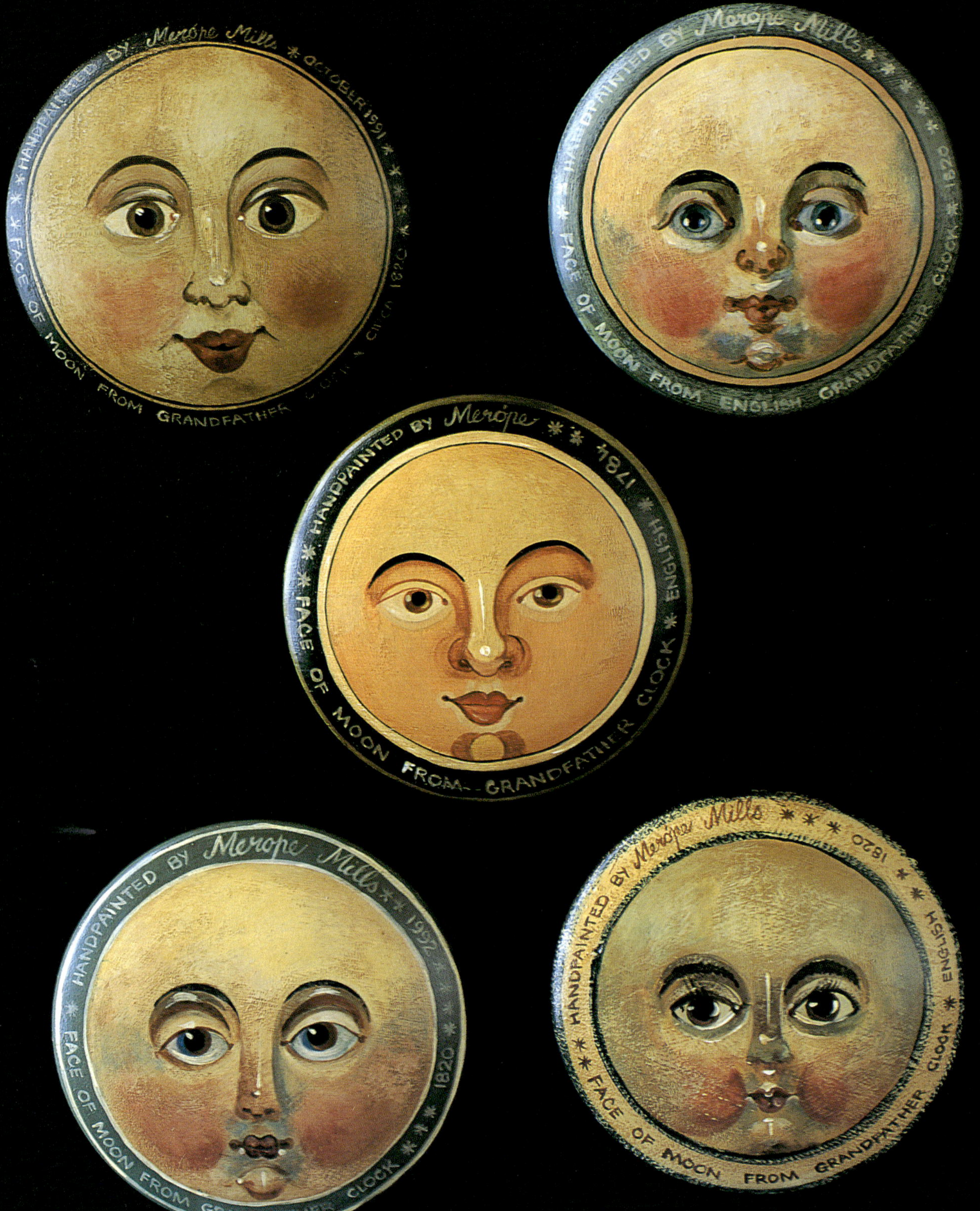

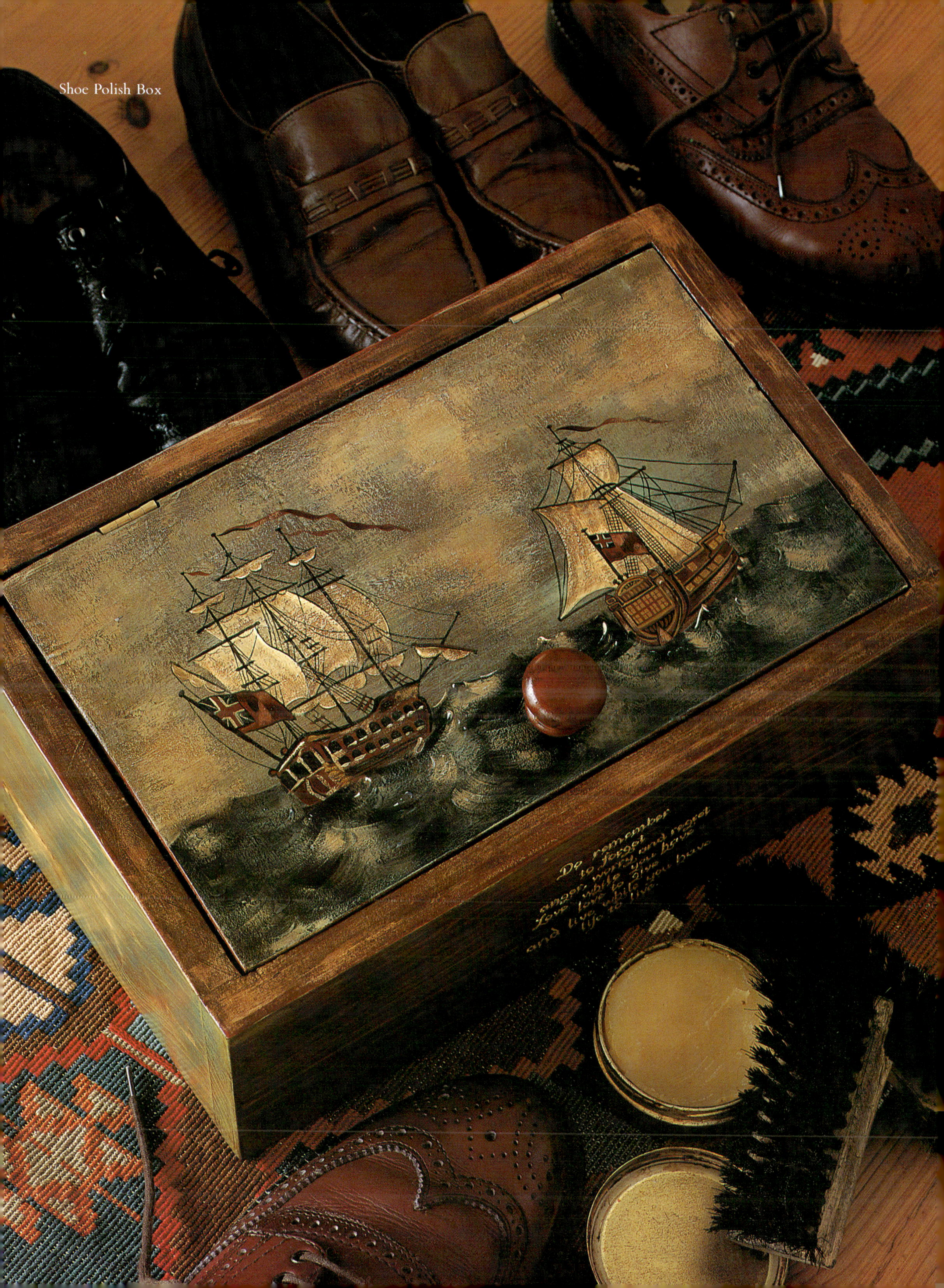

Shoe Polish Box

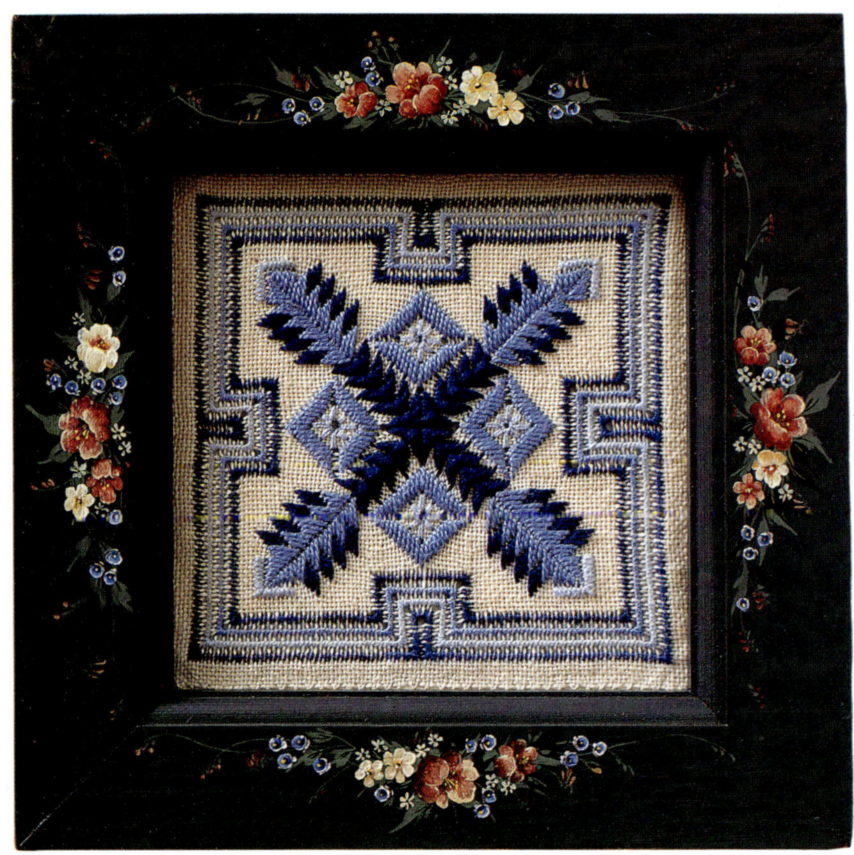

Frame for Embroidery

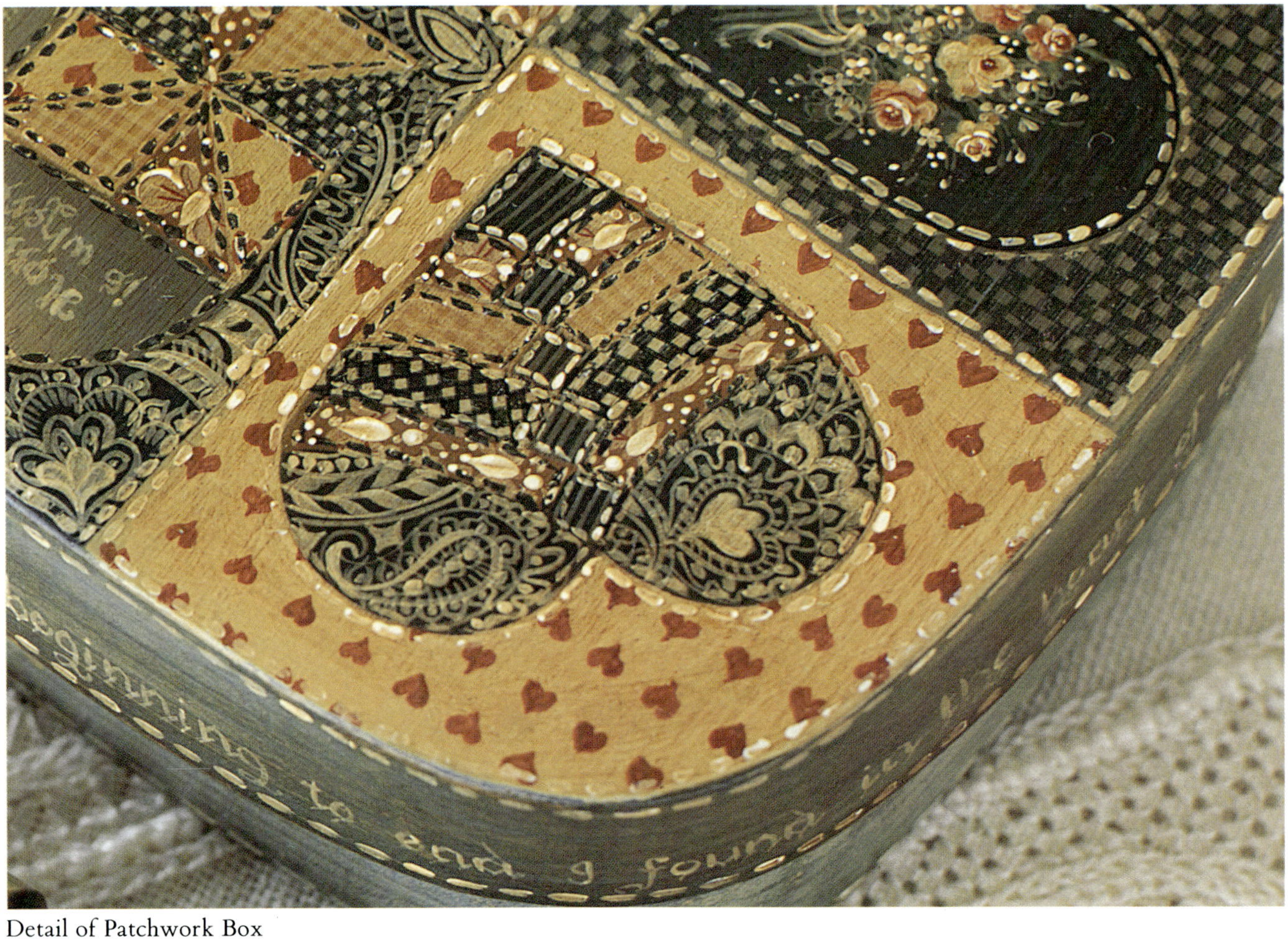

Detail of Patchwork Box

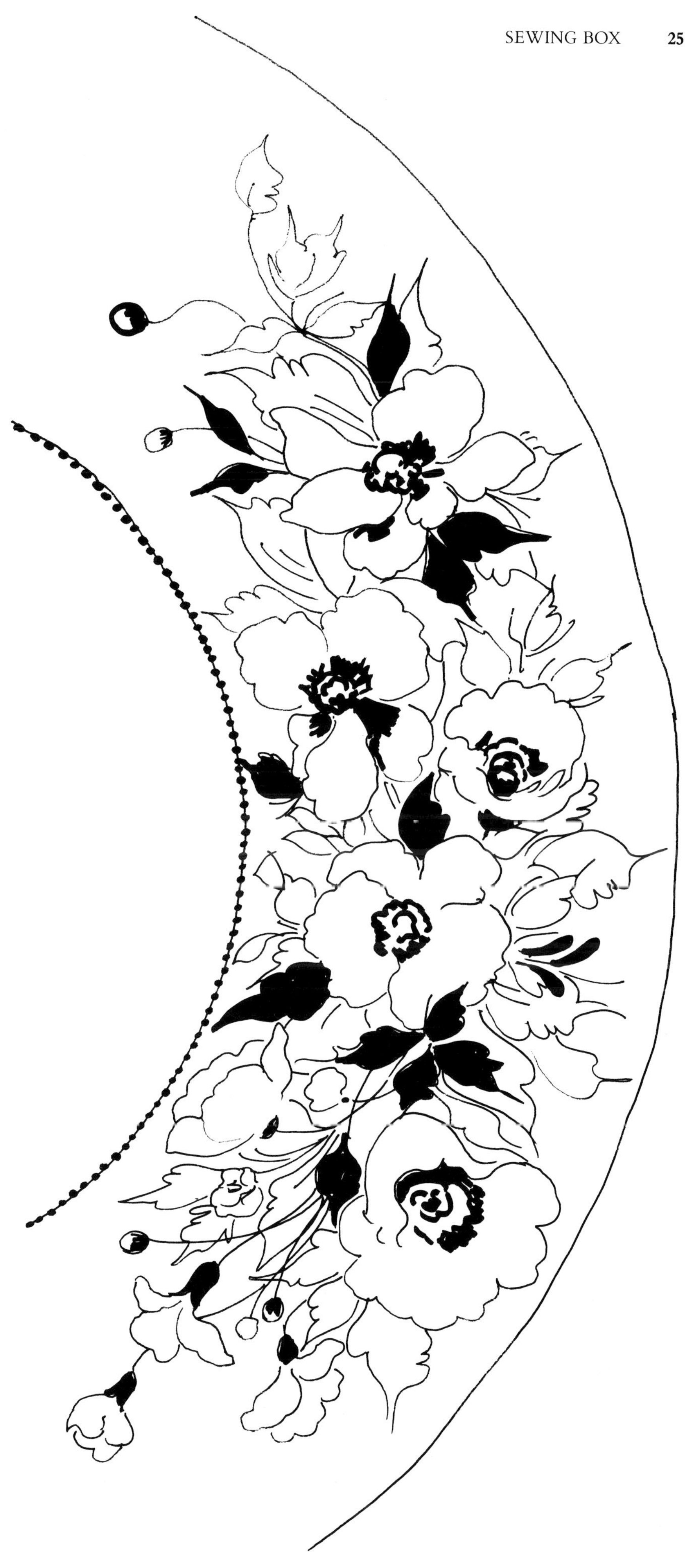

Antique Post Card Box

Letter writing is the only device
for combining solitude and good company.

Lord Byron

Requirements:
You will need an oval box measuring 36 cm by 16 cm (15⅜ inches x 6⅛ inches), as well as an old pansy post card with a written message on the back.

Brushes: Raphael No. 2
Large flat brush for the background

Palette: Jo Sonja's — French Blue
Black
Warm White
Green Oxide
Diox Purple
Red Earth
Burgundy
Fawn
Smoked Pearl
Carbon Black
Cadmium Yellow Mid

Matisse — Burgundy or Jo Sonja's Burgundy plus Carbon Black (mixed 10:1)

Jo Sonja's All-Purpose Sealer or Matisse Sealer

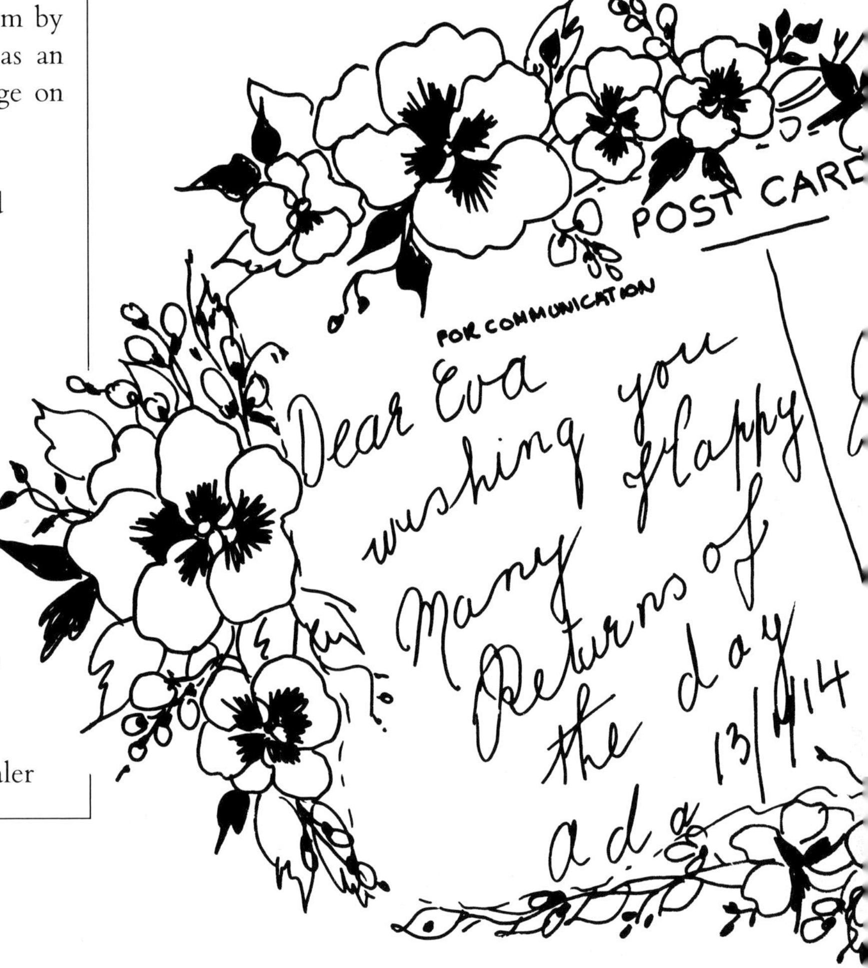

This project includes découpage of a post card, which must be completed before further work is undertaken.

First trace positioning of card on the post card box using graphite paper and stylus.

Working on a piece of plastic, put the card flat down with the picture upwards. With your finger, smooth the entire card with a thin, smooth layer of sealer in a horizontal direction. Start from the top, working from left to right. Go over the edges of the card onto the plastic so as not to build up sealer on the edges. Lift the card carefully and let it dry. (You don't want it sticking to the plastic.)

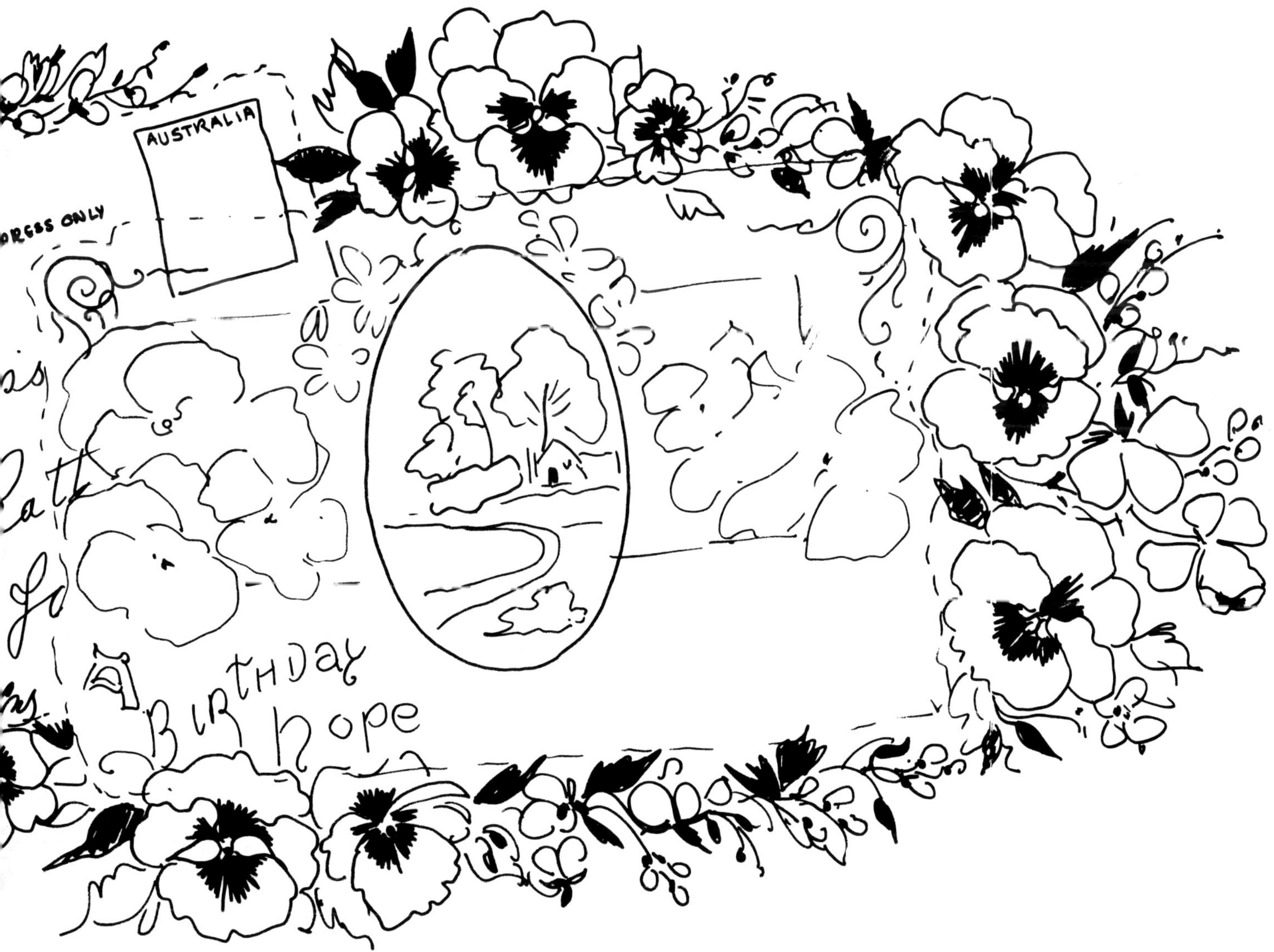

When the first coat is dry apply the sealer vertically, smoothing from top to bottom.

Alternate directions until the card has six coats. Dry between each coat.

Then turn the card over and, with the writing side upwards, apply four alternate coats of sealer, drying in between.

Cut off a thin border all around the card with scissors. Soak the card in warm to hot water for a day or two. The card will go milky, but don't worry, as it dries clear.

Remove the card from the water and carefully edge your nail in between the back and front of the card and slowly split it in two.

Place the right side of picture card on a hard surface (workbench) and rub off excess paper with your thumb. You might need a little water as you are rubbing.

Repeat this with the written side of card. Rinse them under a tap to remove fluffy bits of paper and let them dry flat on a tea towel.

Place your cards on the box. The written side should be stuck down first. Pick it up and apply sealer all over the back and front of card making sure the edges are well covered. Position it on your box according to the tracings. Working from the centre of card slowly push out towards the edges so removing all bubbles and getting it as smooth as possible. Wipe the excess sealer off with a damp cloth.

Apply the picture side in the same way. Let them both dry (at least a day and a night).

With sandpaper sand the edges until smooth.

PREPARATION

Now the box is ready to be treated as for other projects.

- Paint a wash from the edge of the cards to the outer edge of the box. I used a wash of French Blue and Carbon Black.
- Paint the rest of the box with this mixture, keeping it watery. When dry, sand along the grain.

METHOD

- Leaves:
  Paint leaves free hand all around cards, so forming a background for the pansies, using watery Green Oxide.
- Pansies:

a. Trace pansies on box.

b. Base coat pansies in Smoked Pearl.

c. Mix Red Earth and Diox Purple together. Paint the back petals in this colour. By adding Fawn to this colour you can shade the petals towards the centre.

d. At the base of the petals fan out strokes of Carbon Black.

e. The next two side petals are painted in a mixture of Warm White with a touch of Cadmium Yellow and Fawn. At the base you repeat the Carbon Black strokes.

f. The last middle petal is painted in a mixture of Red Earth and Jo Sonja's Burgundy. Fan out the Carbon Black in the centre.

g. In very thick Warm White add two little side commas on the side petals and a Cadmium Yellow Mid centre.

- All buds are done in a watery Red Earth with a sideload of Matisse Burgundy.
- Calyxes and stems are painted in Green Oxide plus Carbon Black. Add darker leaves and finer stems around the box.
- Paint a thin line just inside the edge of top of lid in a mixture of Red Earth and Burgundy.
- In the same colour paint a broader line then a fine line above the edge of the rim of the box.
- I painted a verse on the rim in Warm White.

  What lies behind us and what lies before us
  are tiny matters compared to what lies within us.
  R.W. Emerson

- Antique.
- Varnish.

MOON BROOCHES

Take time ...
to love
the little things.

Requirements:
You will need a wooden brooch 7.5 cm (3 inches) in diameter.
Brush: Raphael No. 2
Palette: Jo Sonja's — Yellow Oxide
Warm White
Red Earth
Carbon Black
Green Oxide
Moss Green
Burnt Sienna
Fawn

Matisse — Burgundy or Jo Sonja's Burgundy plus Carbon Black (mixed 10:1)

PREPARATION
Two coats of Smoked Pearl.

METHOD

- Measure circles from diagram and draw them in with a good compass.
- The inner circle is the face of the moon. Paint the upper half with Yellow Oxide mixed with Warm White. Paint the lower half with Yellow Oxide plus Red Earth and Warm White.
- Blend with a dry brush where the two shades meet so there's no definite line.
- Paint Warm White between circles 1 and 2.

- Outline circle 1 in Black.
- Paint Carbon Black between circles 2 and 3.
- Mix Green Oxide and Moss Green together and paint between line 3 and end of brooch.
- Trace face on brooch.
- Paint forehead and nose in a mixture of Yellow Oxide and Warm White.
- Paint above eyelids and down sides of nose and either side of chin in Burnt Sienna with Red Earth and Fawn.
- Paint around nostrils in a darker shade of this mixture.
- Outline nostrils and outer edge of nose in Jo Sonja's Burgundy.
- Paint a line and a dot down the centre of nose in Warm White. Refer to photograph for further details.
- Paint eyelids and under eyes in a mixture of Warm White and Yellow Oxide.
- White of eyes is Warm White.
- Iris is Burnt Sienna.
- Pupil is Carbon Black.
- Outline lower part of lid in Burgundy, the upper part in Burnt Sienna.
- Put a white dot on left side of pupils and a small Yellow Oxide comma on the lower right side of pupils.
- Paint the mouth in a watery mixture of Red Earth and Burgundy.
- Outline the mouth and centre line with Matisse Burgundy.
- Outline arch of chin in Burnt Sienna.
- Paint the eyebrows Carbon Black.
- Paint the words in Warm White in the black rim of the brooch:
  Face of Moon from Grandfather Clock
  English 1784
- Antique.
- Varnish.

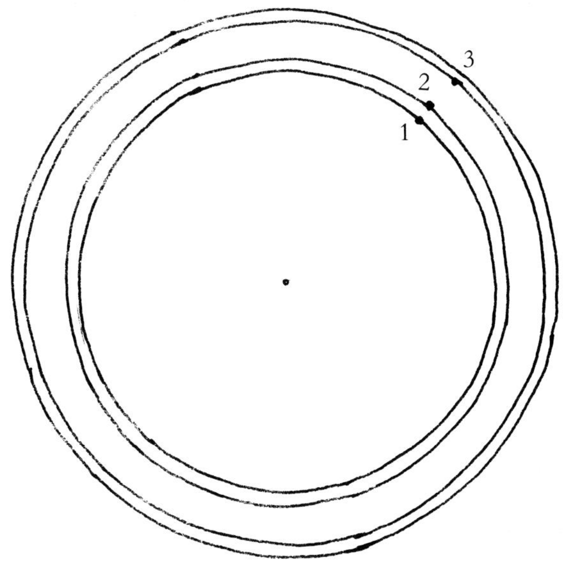

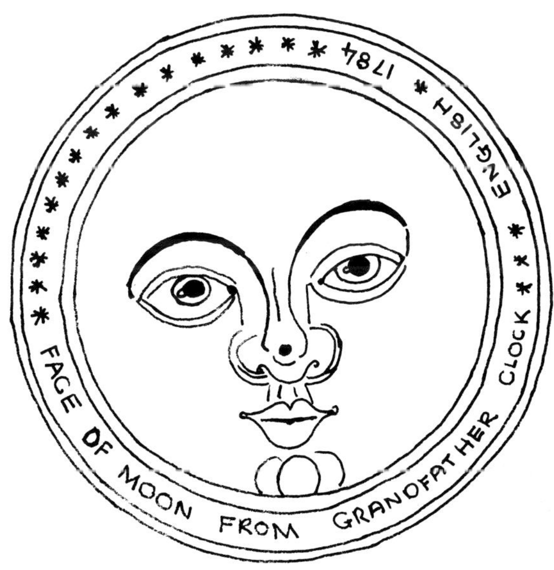

Shoe Polish Box

'The time has come', the Walrus said,
'To talk of many things:
Of shoes — and ships — and sealing wax —
of cabbages — and kings —
And why the sea is boiling hot —
and whether pigs have wings.'

Lewis Carroll

Requirements:
You will need a wooden box 36.5 cm x 23 cm (12⅞ inches x 7½ inches).
Brushes: Raphael No. 2 or No. 3
Flat brush 1″ wide
Flat brush ¼″ wide
Palette: Jo Sonja's — Smoked Pearl
Warm White
Sapphire Blue
Storm Blue
Red Earth
Burgundy
Carbon Black
Yellow Oxide
Provincial Beige
Matisse — Burgundy or Jo Sonja's Burgundy plus Carbon Black (mixed 10:1)
Antique Green or Jo Sonja's Teal Green plus Fawn (mixed 1:1)

PREPARATION

- On the lid, use the large flat brush to paint two coats of Smoked Pearl. Three quarters of the lid is the sky and one quarter the sea.
- Paint the sky with thick Warm White to which no water has been added. Strokes should be straight across and straight down, to form a textured look.
- Mix Sapphire Blue and Antique Green and add to the sky, covering a little section at a time. Slowly build up a canvas-type texture by adding Blue/Green mixture, then Warm White, then Blue/Green again.
- The sea is painted in the same manner using a colour combination of Antique Green and Storm Blue. The waves are added afterwards.
- The rest of the box is painted with Moss Green and Sapphire Blue. When dry it is sanded with water and Wet and Dry sandpaper. You can remove as much paint as you wish, so exposing the wood grain.

METHOD

- Trace Stage 1 design of both ships onto the lid of the box.
- Squeeze out Warm White and let it stand a little to thicken. Paint all sails, both open and furled in both ships.
- Give them a second coat.
- Mix Red Earth with a little of Jo Sonja's Burgundy and paint in all flags and base of ships.
- In Ship A paint all detail in Carbon Black.
- In Ship B paint all detail in Yellow Oxide.
- Shade the sails using the Dry Brush Method.

Ship A
The shading and texture work is done in the following colours and combinations of colours: Provincial Beige, Black, Warm White. Refer to photograph for details. The folded sails have a touch of Red Earth.

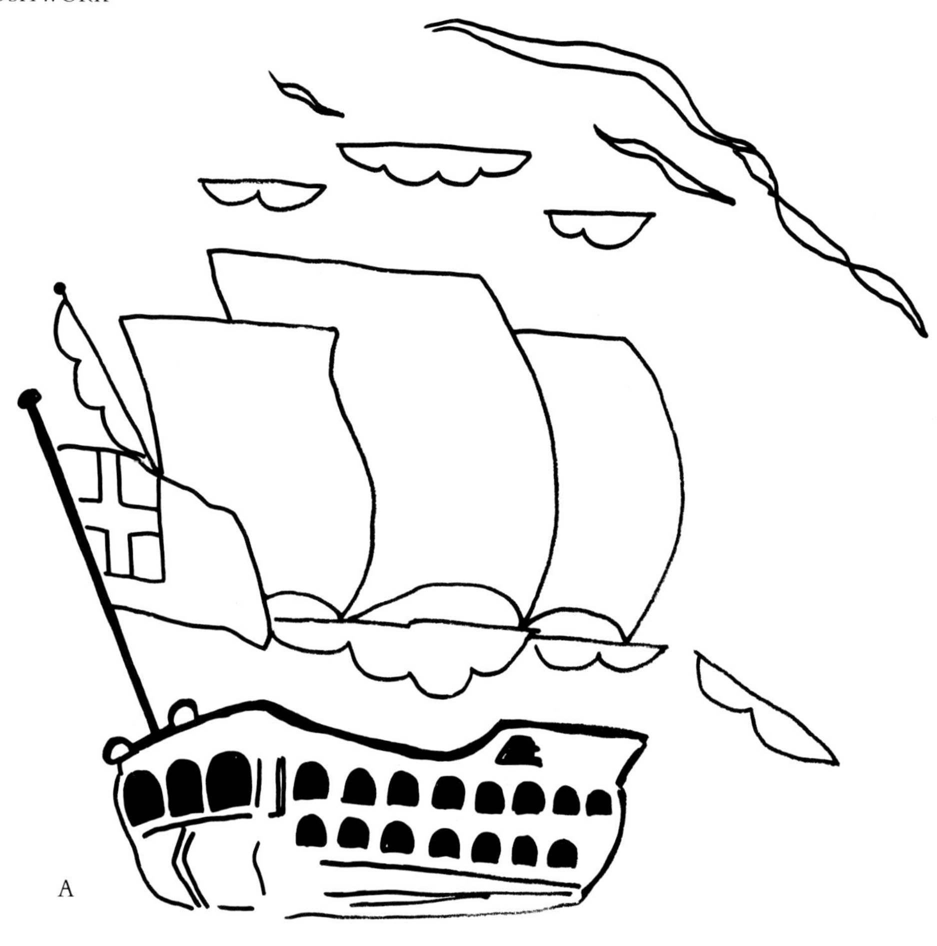

A

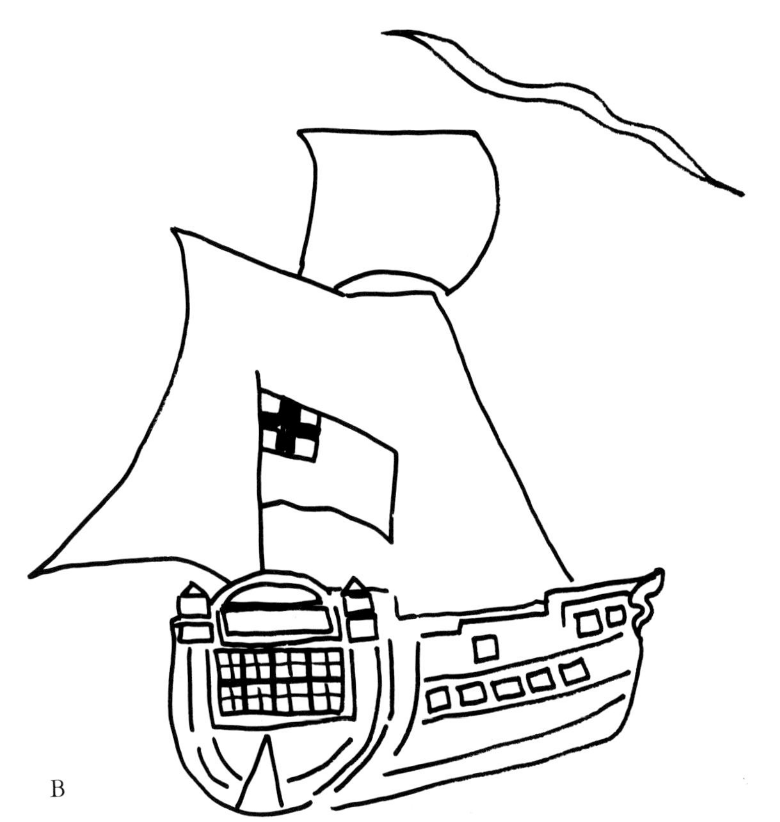

B

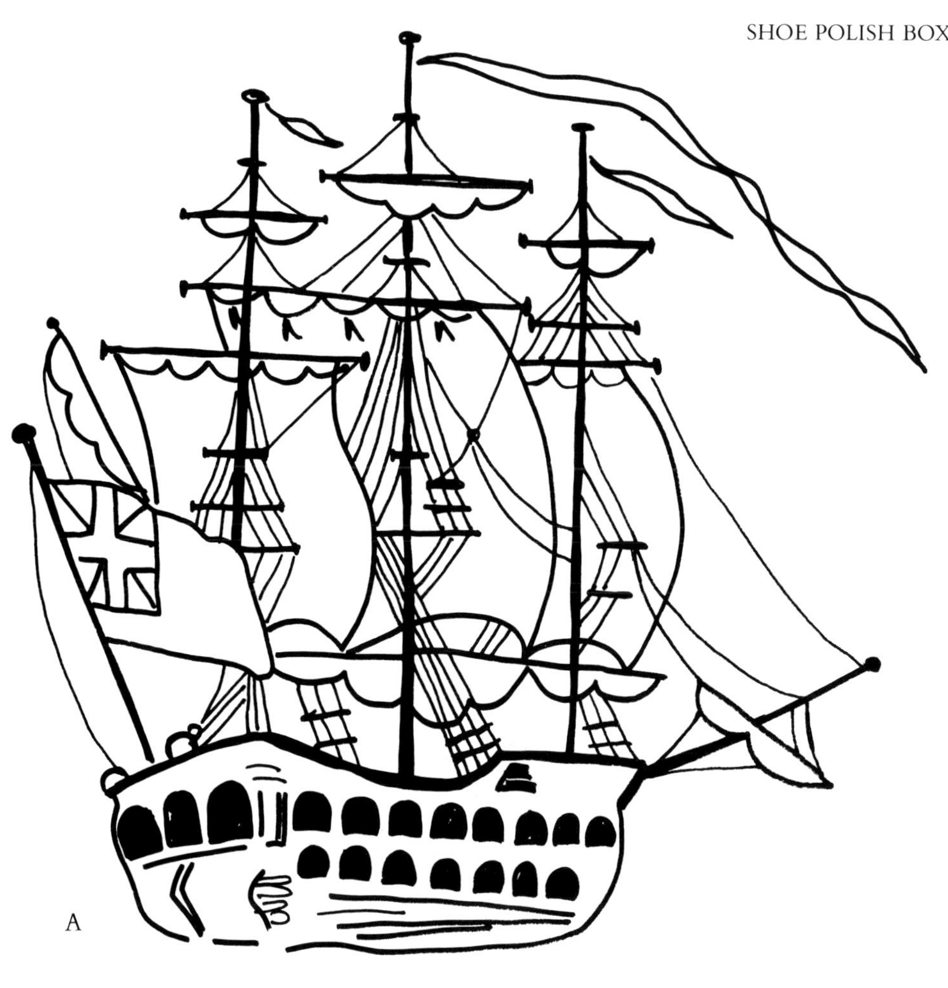

A

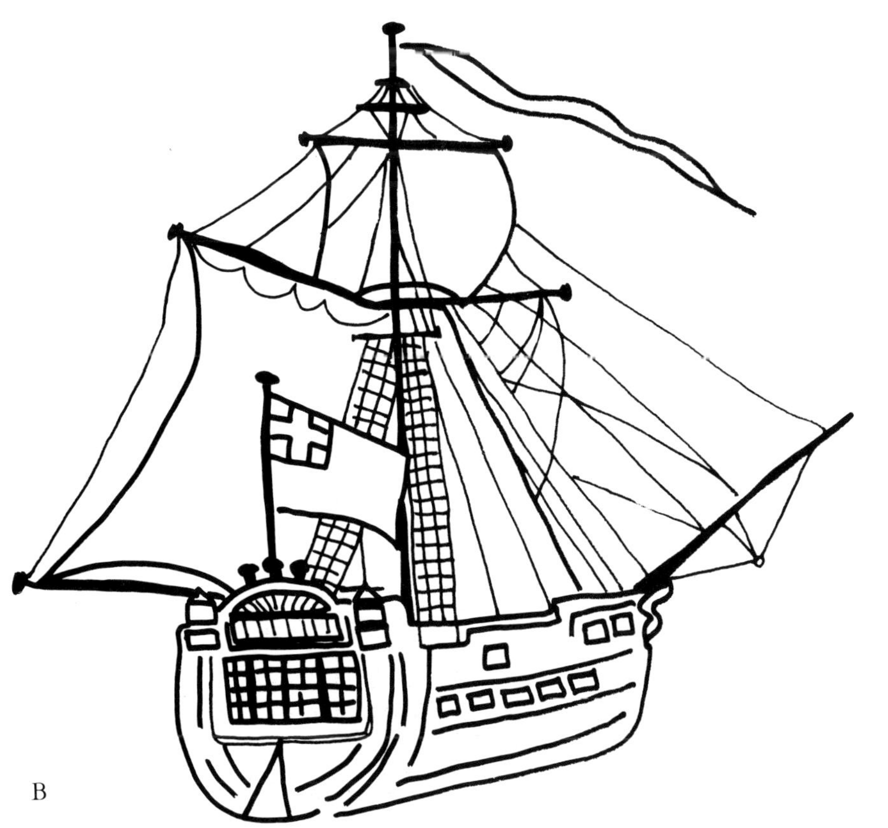

B

Ship B
The shading is done with Provincial Beige for the darker folds and Yellow Oxide plus Warm White for the rest.

- Trace Stage 2 over the ships.
- Paint all poles and lines in Carbon Black.
- The two large flags have a Burgundy cross, outlined with a Warm White line. The corners are painted with Storm Blue.
- Shading of the flags — the darker folds are in Matisse Burgundy and the highlights are Warm White. Use the Dry Brush Technique.
- Add Warm White, Yellow Oxide and Carbon Black to the detail of the base of the ships.
- The sea is painted with the ¼″ flat brush in Storm Blue then Warm White. The brush strokes should imitate the up and down movement of small choppy waves.
- The border and knob are painted in Red Earth plus Burgundy. Add the Warm White using the Dry Brush Method once the Red Earth has dried.
- The following verse is written on the front side of the box in Warm White.
  Do remember
  to forget
  anger, worry and regret.
  Love while you have
  love to give
  and live while you have
  life to live.
- Antique.
- Varnish.

FRAME FOR EMBROIDERY

God could not be everywhere,
so He made mothers.

Proverb

The embroidery within the frame was stitched by my mother.

Requirements:
You will need a frame 21.5 cm (8½ inches) square.
Brush: Raphael No. 1
Palette: Jo Sonja's — Smoked Pearl
Teal Green
Carbon Black
Plum Pink
Fawn
Burgundy
Yellow Light
Yellow Oxide
Warm White
Sapphire Blue
Diox Purple
French Blue
Matisse — Antique Green or Jo Sonja's Teal Green plus Fawn (mixed 1:1)

PREPARATION

Sand the frame and paint two coats of French Blue.

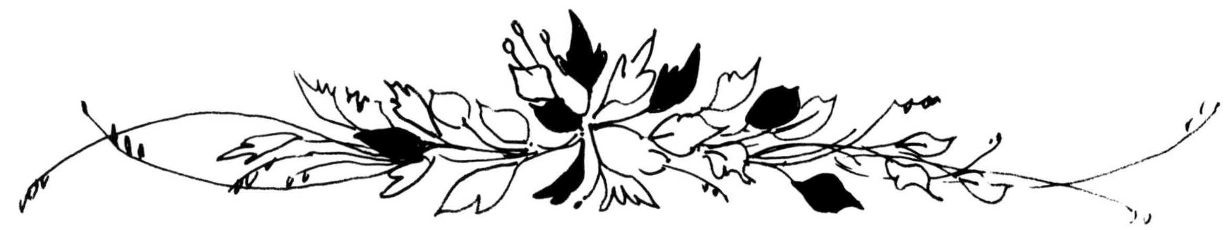

METHOD

- Trace the leaf design four times around the frame with white graphite paper and a stylus.
- Mix Antique Green with Smoked Pearl and paint in leaves and stems.
- Mix Teal Green with Carbon Black and paint in the dark leaves.
- Trace in the flowers.
- Give the two roses and two large daisies a base coat of Smoked Pearl.
- Mix Plum Pink, Fawn and Smoked Pearl and paint both roses with this pale pink.
- When dry pull the Smoked Pearl from outer edge of the top petals and upper edge of the three bottom petals. Shade the centre and lower edge of the bottom petals with Burgundy.
- The stamens are Smoked Pearl with a Yellow Light dot at the end.

- Mix Yellow Oxide and Smoked Pearl and paint two large daisies. Pull Warm White from outer edge of the petals in towards the centre.
- The centre is a Burgundy half circle with a White dot in the middle.
- The small daisies are Smoked Pearl with a Black centre.
- Mix Sapphire Blue, Warm White and a touch of Diox Purple together. Load the brush in this colour and pick up a sideload of White. With the sideload facing upwards paint a half circle. In the centre paint a dot of Diox Purple and a Yellow Light Dot on top of that.
- With a clean brush pick up Warm White and complete the little circle with tiny little commas coming across.
- The freesias are straight commas in Plum Pink with a sideload of Burgundy.
- Varnish.

NEEDLECASE

But here the needle plies its busy task
The pattern grows, the well-depict'd flower
Unfold its bosom, buds and leaves and sprigs,
And curling tendrils, gracefully disposed,
Follow the nimble fingers of the fair;
A wreath that cannot fade, of flowers that blow
With most success when all besides decay.

William Cowper. 1784

Requirements:
You will need a 14 cm (5½ inch) wooden needlecase.
Brush: Raphael No. 1 or No. 0
Palette: Jo Sonja's — Green Oxide
Teal Green
Smoked Pearl
Fawn
Plum Pink
Warm White
Burgundy
Yellow Oxide

PREPARATION

Give a watery Smoked Pearl wash over the case so that the lovely wood grain still shows through the paint.

METHOD

- Paint leaves in Green Oxide with a sideload of Teal Green. Paint in the fine trailing stems of the freesias. You will do two designs in front and two repeated at the back (four posies in total).
- Paint the roses as follows: First, give them a base coat of Smoked Pearl. Then mix a pale pink from Fawn, a touch of Plum Pink, then add Warm White. Coat the roses with this colour, over the Smoked Pearl.

  Now add a darker shade of pink (Fawn and Plum Pink) in the centre, around the bowl of the roses and on some of the petals (as shown in the illustration).

  Last, add Warm White, as thick as possible, in circular little strokes. Add a touch of Burgundy to the centre and paint in a few dots for the stamens in Warm White.

  Paint in dots of the darker pink at the ends of the trailing stems.
- The daisies are painted in Warm White with Yellow Oxide centres.
- You can enhance the borders by painting them in the pale pink.
- Varnish.

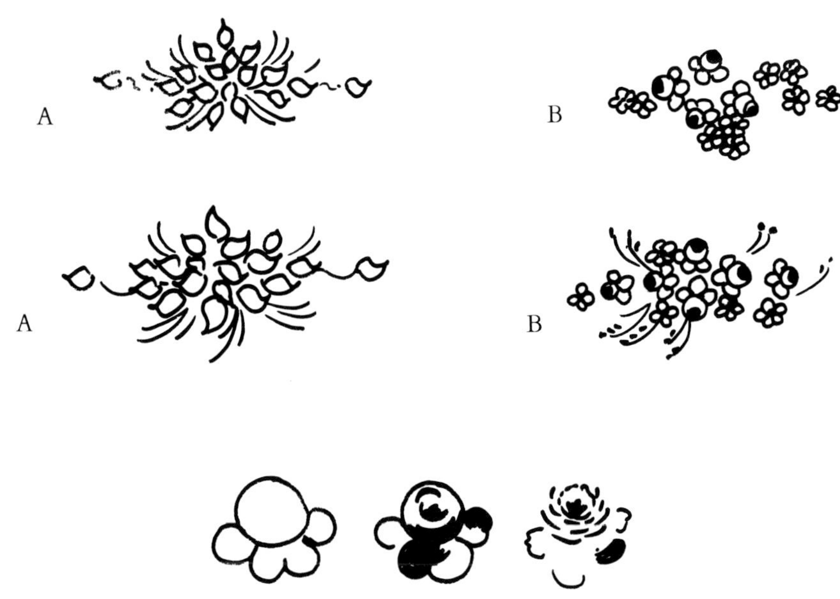

IRON POT

Earth laughs in flowers
Ralph Waldo Emerson

Brushes: Raphael No. 3 and 5
Palette: Jo Sonja's — French Blue
Warm White
Green Oxide
Moss Green
Teal Green
Carbon Black
Smoked Pearl
Burgundy
Diox Purple
Red Earth
Cadmium Yellow Mid
Matisse — Burgundy or Jo Sonja's Burgundy plus Carbon Black (mixed 10:1)

PREPARATION

I had this old preserving pot sand-blasted to remove all traces of rust and then had it painted with a 'Stop Rust' paint.

METHOD

Mix a little French Blue to Warm White and paint the top of the pot with this light colour. Add more French Blue and gradually work your way down the pot until only French Blue is used at the bottom.

- Trace the pansies and leaves with a stylus and graphite paper. I have given you only a section of the pattern. This section could be repeated along the pot.
- Leaves:
  Using a Raphael No. 5 brush, paint one side of the leaf in Green Oxide with a sideload of Moss Green. The other side is painted in Teal Green with a sideload of Teal mixed with Carbon Black.
  The brush strokes are commas coming in towards the centre vein, as shown in the illustration.
- Pansies:
  Raphael No. 5 or No. 3 brush.
  All pansies are base-coated in Smoked Pearl. If they are still transparent, give them a second coat.
  All the centres of the pansies are done in the following way: Paint a half circle below in Cadmium Yellow Mid, then Green Oxide in the middle and two Warm White commas sitting off the middle petals.

a. Pansy No 1:
Mix together Jo Sonja's Burgundy and Diox Purple. Paint a petal at a time and each time lift some of the paint with a clean brush, so highlighting the petal. The centre of the petals are painted in a mixture Black and Diox Purple as in the illustration.
Outline petals with a fine line of Warm White.
Paint in the centre as explained above.

b. Pansy No 2:
The back two petals are painted in a mixture of Jo Sonja's Burgundy and Diox Purple with a Cadmium Yellow Mid centre.
The two side petals have Burgundy and Purple on the outer edge, then Cadmium Yellow Mid and then a Black and Burgundy centre. A touch of Jo Sonja's Burgundy can be added where the Black mixture meets the yellow.

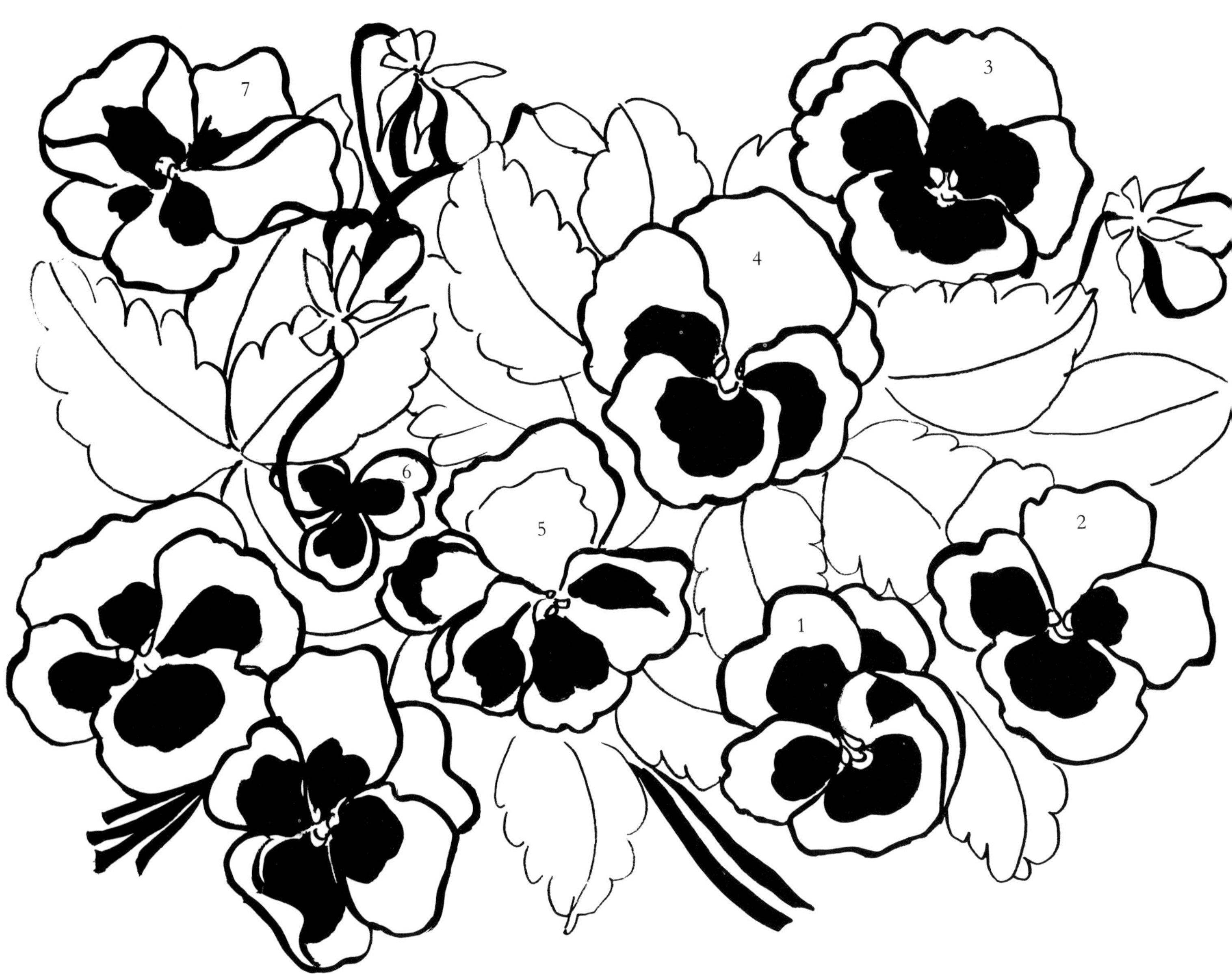
7
3
4
6
5
2
1

The centre bottom petal has Cadmium Yellow Mid on the outer edge and a Black and Burgundy centre. Again add a touch of Jo Sonja's Burgundy where the two colours meet.

Outline petals with Warm White.

Paint in the centre as explained above.

c. Pansy No 3:
Paint the back two petals in Purple and Burgundy, lifting some of the paint and so highlighting the petals. This is done by cleaning the brush and going back and removing some of the paint.

Paint a Black and Purple centre.

To paint the two sides of the petals you start with Warm White on the outer edge, then Jo Sonja's Burgundy and then into the centre of Black and Purple.

The centre bottom petal is a mixture of Purple and Burgundy on the outer edge, then Burgundy and then into Black and Purple.

Paint in the centre as explained above.

d. Pansy No 4:
The top two petals are painted in Jo Sonja's Burgundy and then Cadmium Yellow Mid.

The two side petals and middle bottom one are painted in Cadmium Yellow Mid with Warm White on the outer edge with a centre of Black and Matisse Burgundy. Where the two colours meet, a bit of Jo Sonja's Burgundy is added.

Paint in the centre as explained above.

e. Pansy No 5:
The upper petal is Cadmium Yellow Mid and is blended into a mixture of Purple and Matisse Burgundy.

The left side petal is Purple with Matisse Burgundy and highlighted by lifting some of the paint.

The same combinations apply to the other petals. Finish off with a fine line of Warm White around the petals.

f. Pansy No 6:
The petals are painted in Cadmium Yellow Mid with Warm White. The centres are Black and Matisse Burgundy.

g. Pansy No 7:
The two bottom petals are Matisse Burgundy with Purple. Lift some paint off to add shading and where the petal folds up use the colours solid.
The two side petals are Warm White with a touch of Yellow. Add a Black centre and, when dry, add a touch of Purple with Burgundy to the upper centre of petals.
The top petal is painted in Red Earth with Jo Sonja's Burgundy. Add a Black centre and Warm White line around all the petals.

Repeat the colour variations on the rest of the pansies.

- Go over some of the leaves and overlap some leaves onto the pansies. Add clusters of stems at the bottom. Paint in buds and calyxes.
- Antique.
- Varnish.

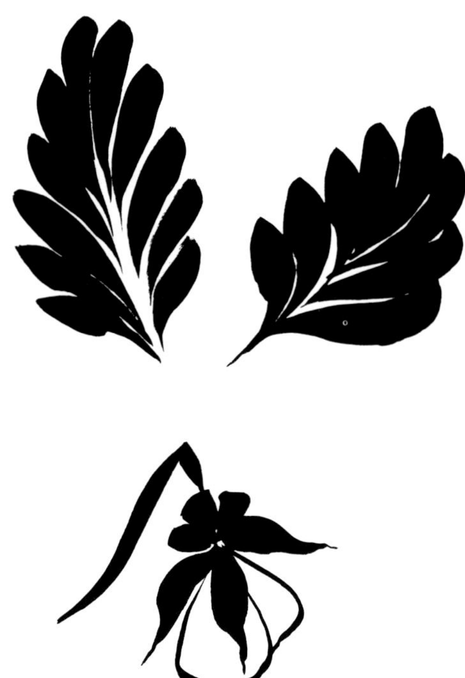

Cottage Plaque

The perfume of the wind-blown flowers,
The glowing warmth of summer sun,
A little kindness from a friend,
The daily loaf; some work well done.
My slippers when my feet feel tired,
A favourite book, some music gay,
The knowledge that God's arms are near!
These things have brought me joy today.

Joyce Frances Carpenter

Requirements:
You will need a wooden plaque 60 cm x 45 cm (23⅝ inches x 17¾ inches)

Brushes: Raphael No. 2, 3 and 5
Raphael Sable No. 2 or 3
Stipple brush or old round brush cut square
Any old round brushes
1 large sea sponge
1 small face sea sponge

Palette: Jo Sonja's — Warm White
Smoked Pearl
French Blue
Yellow Oxide
Green Oxide
Teal Green
Moss Green
Raw Umber
Provincial Beige
Carbon Black
Sapphire Blue
Diox Purple
Plum Pink
Fawn
Red Earth

	Ultramarine Blue
	Turner's Yellow
	Cobolt Blue Hue
	Cadmium Yellow Mid
Matisse —	Burgundy or Jo Sonja's
	Burgundy plus Carbon
	Black (mixed 10:1)

PREPARATION

Give the board two coats of Warm White. Paint on a third coat of Warm White and Smoked Pearl mixed together. While the paint is still wet dip a large (size of a fist) sea sponge into a watery mixture of Warm White and Smoked Pearl and a touch of French Blue (pale blue) and press over the whole plaque.

METHOD

- Trace the outline of the cottage, the scroll and a line where the garland of flowers go (semi-circle) with a stylus and blue graphite paper.
- Within the semi-circle sponge the sky with Warm White using a small face sea sponge.
- Background of Cottage

The distant mountains are painted in watery French Blue.

Next paint the cornfields using a watery mixture of Warm White and Yellow Oxide.

Paint the field in Green Oxide and the bushes in Teal Green.

The trees are sponged with a small face sea sponge in shades of Teal Green, Green Oxide, Moss Green, a mixture of Teal Green and Green Oxide, and Warm White to lighten any of these greens.

The trunks and branches are painted in Raw Umber with a No. 2 brush.

- The Cottage

Trace the cottage back in as your trees would have covered your previous tracings.

Paint the thatch in two coats of thick Provincial Beige.

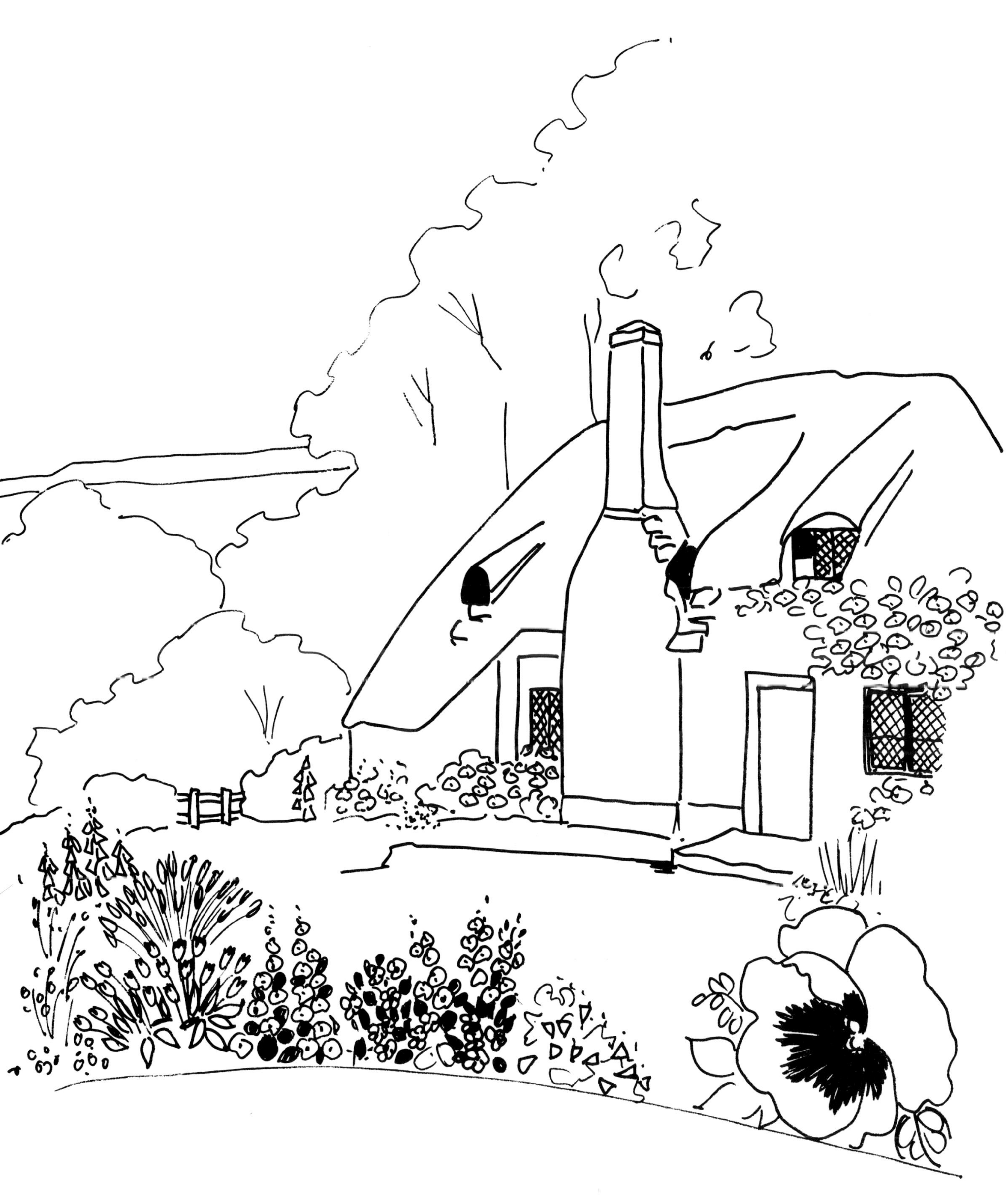

Paint the walls and chimney with two coats of Smoked Pearl.

Paint the path in Yellow Oxide plus Warm White.

Work with a dry brush (use an old Raphael brush) and thick paint to which no water has been added. Mix Raw Umber and Carbon Black together and paint a rough border all around the thatch, also down the sides of humps and parts that fall in the shadow. Mix Provincial Beige and Smoked Pearl and with a dry brush fanned out, pick up paint and lightly brush over roof (Dry Brush Method). In this way you will eventually achieve the look of thatch.

In the same technique pick up Warm White and emphasise humps over windows and the bit running alongside the chimney.

■ Walls and Chimney

With the same Dry Brush Work, build up the texture of the walls and chimney in Smoked Pearl. The walls that project are then highlighted with Warm White, while those in the shadow are painted with a mixture of Smoked Pearl and Provincial Beige. You can also add a shading of Provincial Beige and Sapphire Blue at the bottom of the chimney and wall.

■ Door

The door is painted in Provincial Beige mixed with Sapphire Blue (thick paint). The upper left hand corner is shaded with Carbon Black mixed with Raw Umber.

The bottom of the chimney has a border of Sapphire Blue, plus Provincial Beige, plus a touch of Diox Purple.

■ Windows

The frame is painted in Sapphire Blue mixed with Diox Purple.

The glass is Provincial Beige mixed with Smoked Pearl. The diamond lattice is Raw Umber with Carbon Black.

The cafe curtains are watery Warm White.

Add little diamond shapes of Warm White within the lattice window so giving the effect of glass catching the light.

■ The Garden

The gate on the left side of the house is painted in Raw Umber mixed with Carbon Black.

The shrubs on the left and right of the gate are stippled (with a stipple brush or an old brush cut down square) in different shades of green: Teal Green, Green Oxide, Moss Green.

Paint the lawn in watery Green Oxide.

The creeper over the front door is painted with Teal Green leaves, then Green Oxide leaves, and lastly a mixture of White and Green Oxide leaves.

■ Flowers

a. Roses:

The roses in the creeper over the front door are Plum Pink, a mixture of Plum Pink, Fawn and Warm White, and Warm White.

Load the brush with a pale pink mixture (Plum Pink, Fawn and Warm White). Sideload with Warm White on one side and Plum Pink on the other. With the tip of the brush, paint circular little roses. Repeat roses under the left window.

b. Hollyhocks:

With a mixture of Teal Green and Green Oxide paint in the leaves of Hollyhocks, starting with closed calyxes on top and gradually broadening out into full, open leaves.

Load the brush with a mixture of Cadmium Yellow Mid and Warm White and pick up a sideload of Warm White. Paint the same circles as roses. Dot in a Yellow Oxide centre.

Using the same yellow paint, dot in ground cover here and there.

c. Daisies:

These are next to the left window and in front of the scroll. They are painted with Warm White petals with Cadmium Yellow Mid centres.

d. Snapdragons:

These are planted on the left side of the cottage and in front of the scrolls.

Snapdragons are painted in Red Earth with a sideload of Matisse Burgundy.

Mix Red Earth and Warm White for the centres.

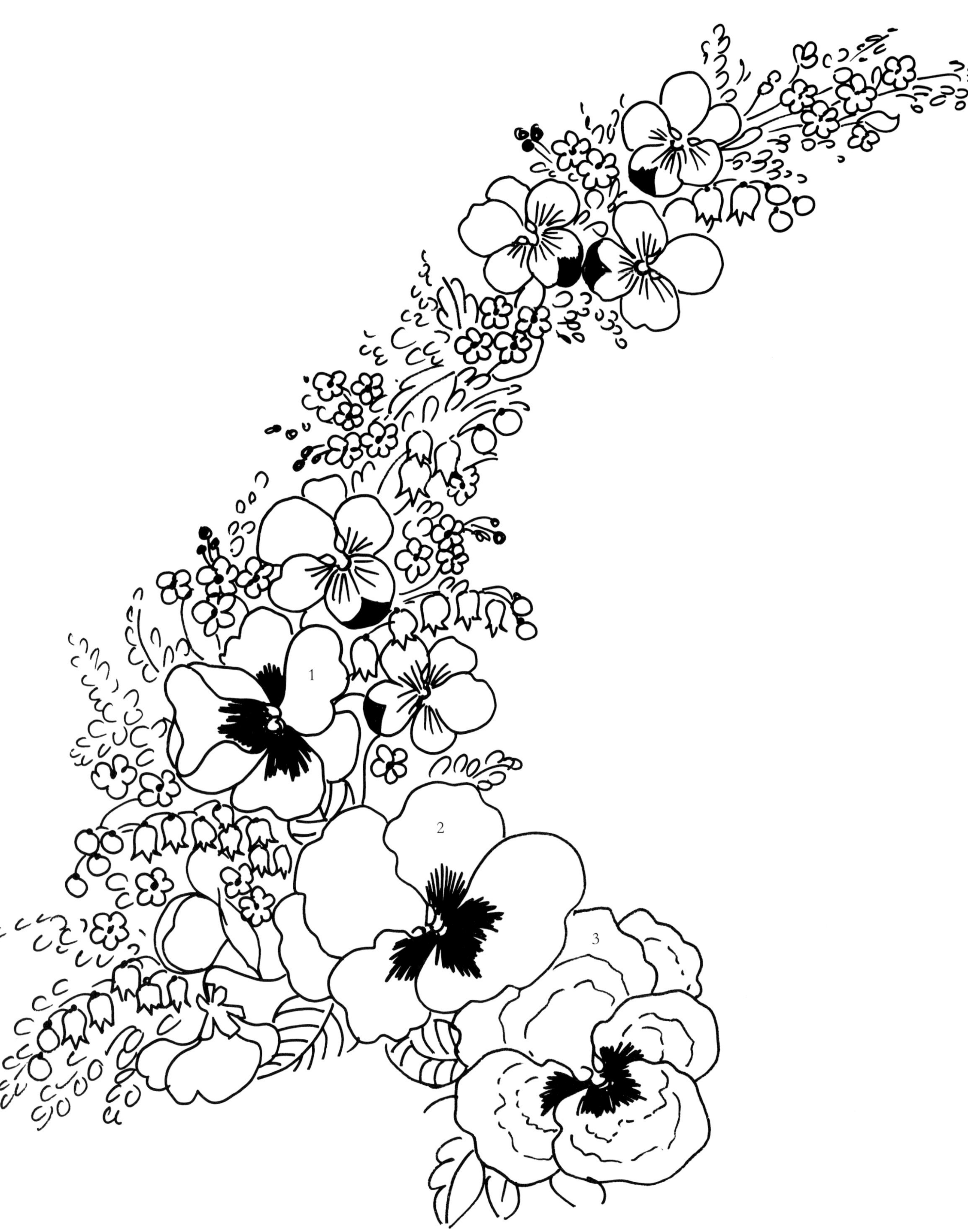
1
2
3

e. Delphiniums:
Start with dots on top of the buds and then fan out with bell-shaped flowers in shades of Sapphire Blue, a mixture of Sapphire Blue and Warm White, and a mixture of Diox Purple and Ultramarine Blue.

f. Lavender:
Paint in the stems that fan out in a bush.

The flowers are painted with the side of your brush making a fine little line. The first set of lines are painted in Diox Purple plus Fawn and Warm White. The second set are paler than the first. To achieve this effect add more White to the first mixture. The third set are painted in Diox Purple with Fawn.

g. Tulips:
These have Teal Green leaves and stems. The flowers are shades of pink (Plum Pink, Warm White and Fawn).

h. Forget-me-nots:
These have Teal Green leaves and stems, with dots of Sapphire Blue, as well as dots of Sapphire Blue plus Warm White.

■ Garland of flowers around cottage

a. The large leaves behind the pansies are painted in shades of Green Oxide, Teal Green and Moss Green. Refer to the method described in Iron Pot (page 43).

b. Base paint all the pansies in Smoked Pearl.

c. Pansy No 1:
Mix Fawn with a touch of Diox Purple and paint the whole pansy.

Load the brush with Warm White and pick up a sideload of thick Warm White. Place the sideload on the outer edge of the petal and go around each petal. Blend Warm White into Purple mixture.

The centre is painted in Black plus Ultramarine Blue. When dry, add Warm White around Black centre.

Add centre as described in the Iron Pot (page 43).

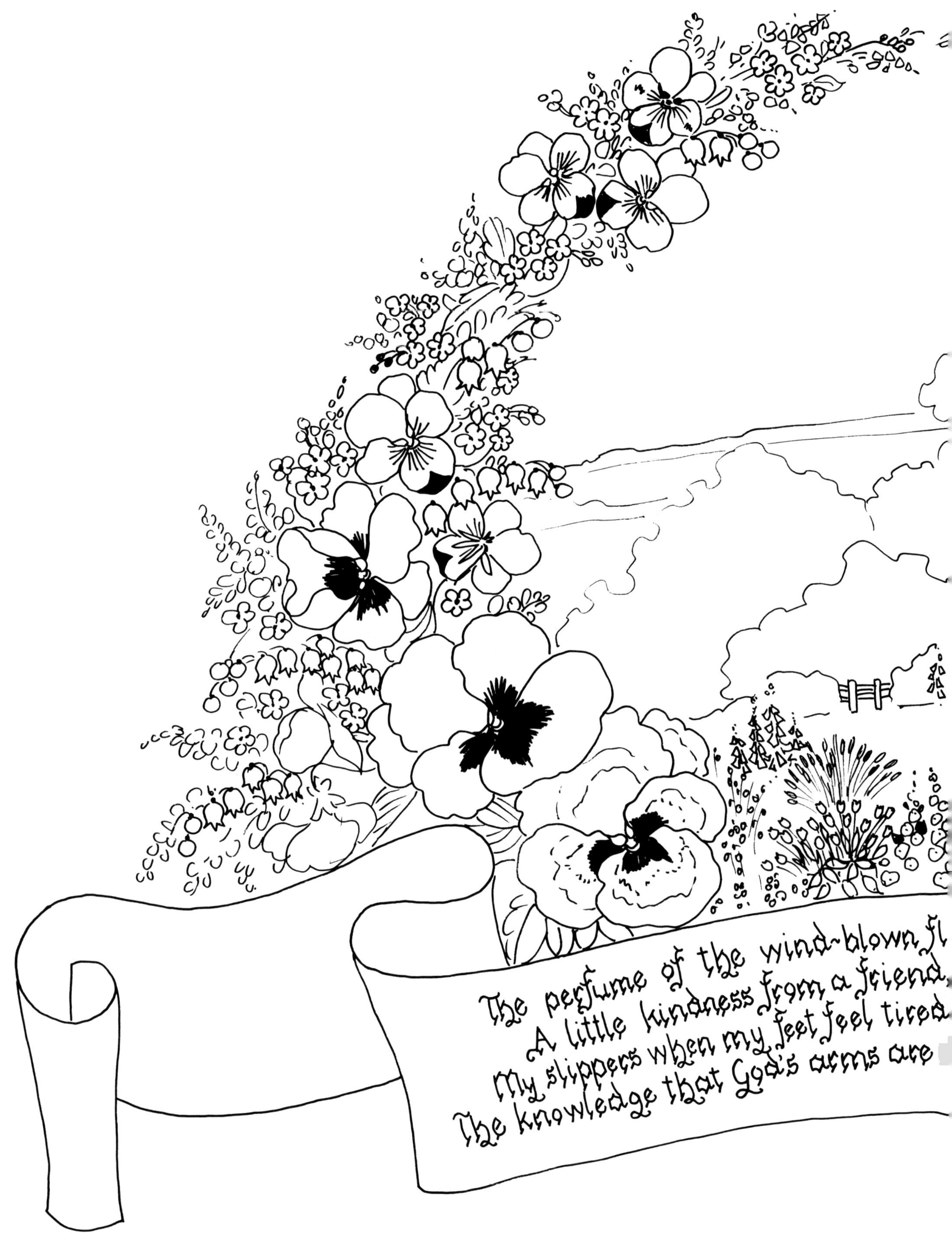
The perfume of the wind-blown fl
A little kindness from a friend,
My slippers when my feet feel tired
The knowledge that God's arms are

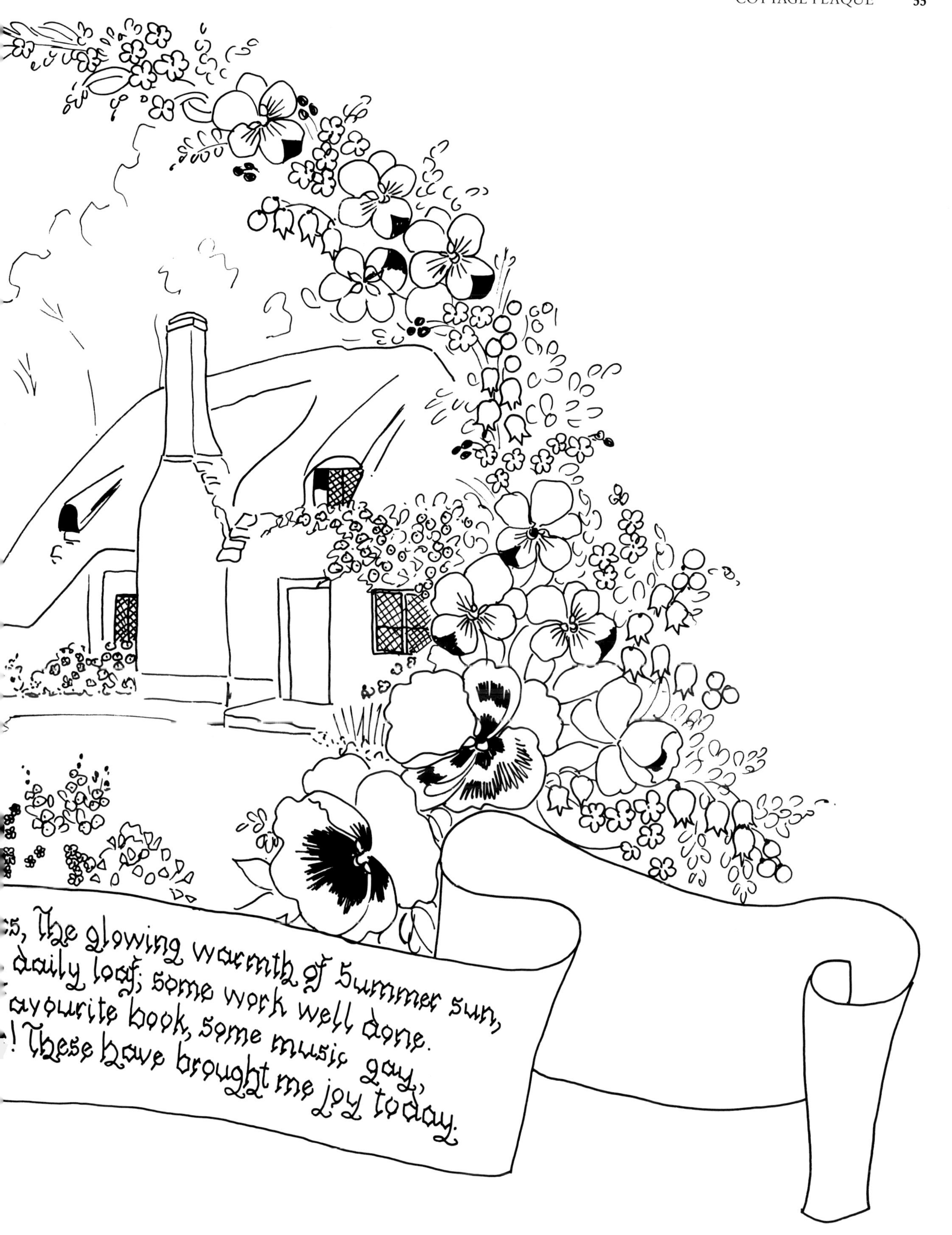
s, The glowing warmth of Summer sun,
daily loaf; some work well done.
avourite book, some music gay,
! These have brought me joy today.

e. Viola:
The two back petals are a mixture of Diox Purple and Matisse Burgundy.

The two side petals are a mixture of Warm White and Turner's Yellow.

The front petals are a mixture of Turner's Yellow and Cadmium Yellow Mid.

The markings are a mixture of Matisse Burgundy and Diox Purple.

Add a centre as in the Iron Pot (page 43).

f. Forget-me-nots:
Paint the five petals in a mixture of Sapphire Blue and Warm White.

The inner five petals are painted in Cobalt Blue Hue.

Use a Yellow Light dot for the centre and Teal Green for the calyxes and stems.

d. Pansies No 2 and 3:
Paint the whole pansy in Turner's Yellow with Warm White. Repeat the procedure with Warm White as described in Pansy No 1.

The centre of the petals are painted with Matisse Burgundy plus Black.

g. Lily-of-the-valley:
Use a very thick Warm White for the buds.

Paint a round circle for the flower and pull down two points on either side and one point in the middle.

The stems are painted in Teal Green.

■ The Scroll

The scroll is painted in a French Blue and Warm White mixture. Highlight with French Blue mixed with more Warm White. The sections of the scroll which are in the shadow are painted in French Blue.

The verse is painted in Warm White.

■ The borders of the plaque are painted in shades of French Blue and Warm White.

■ Antique.

■ Varnish.

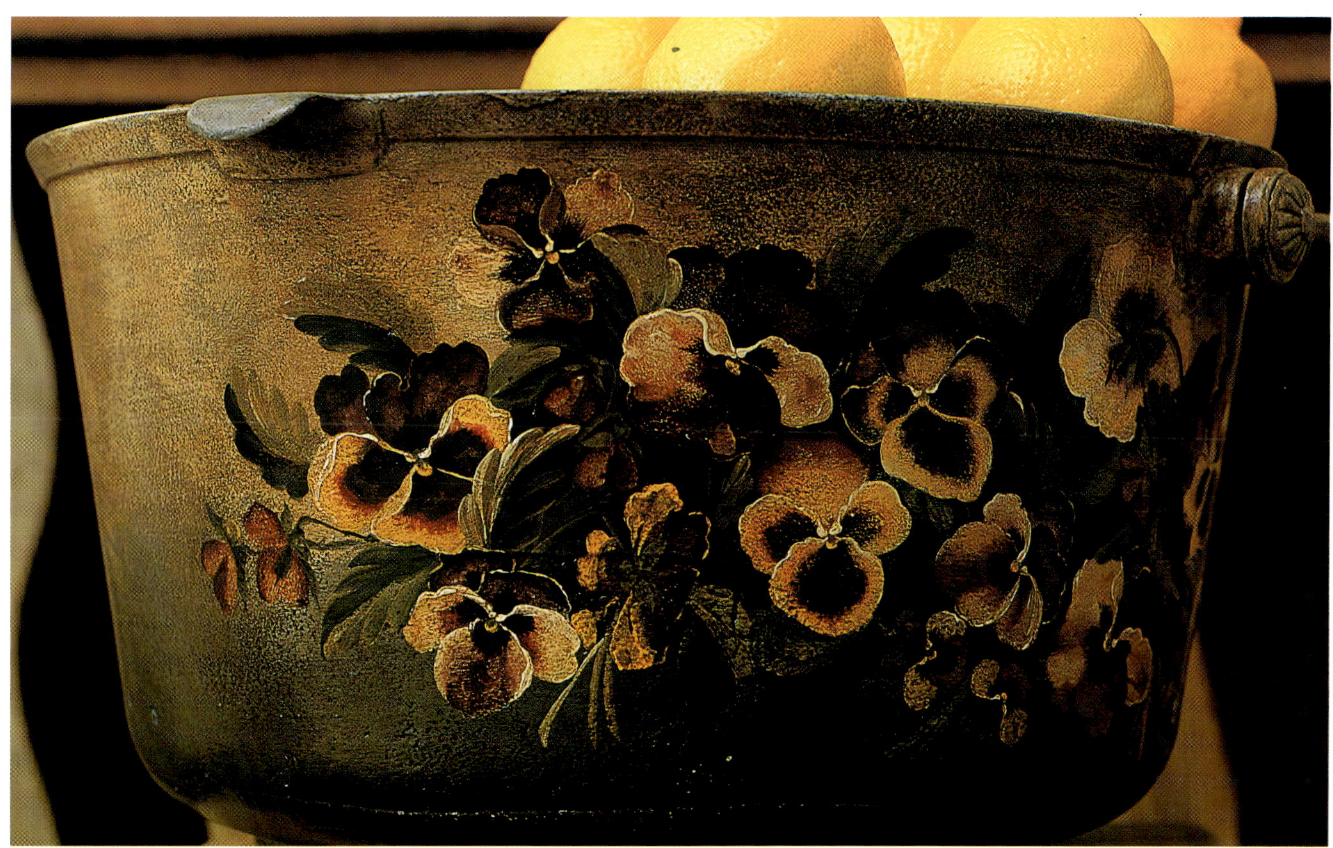

Iron Pot

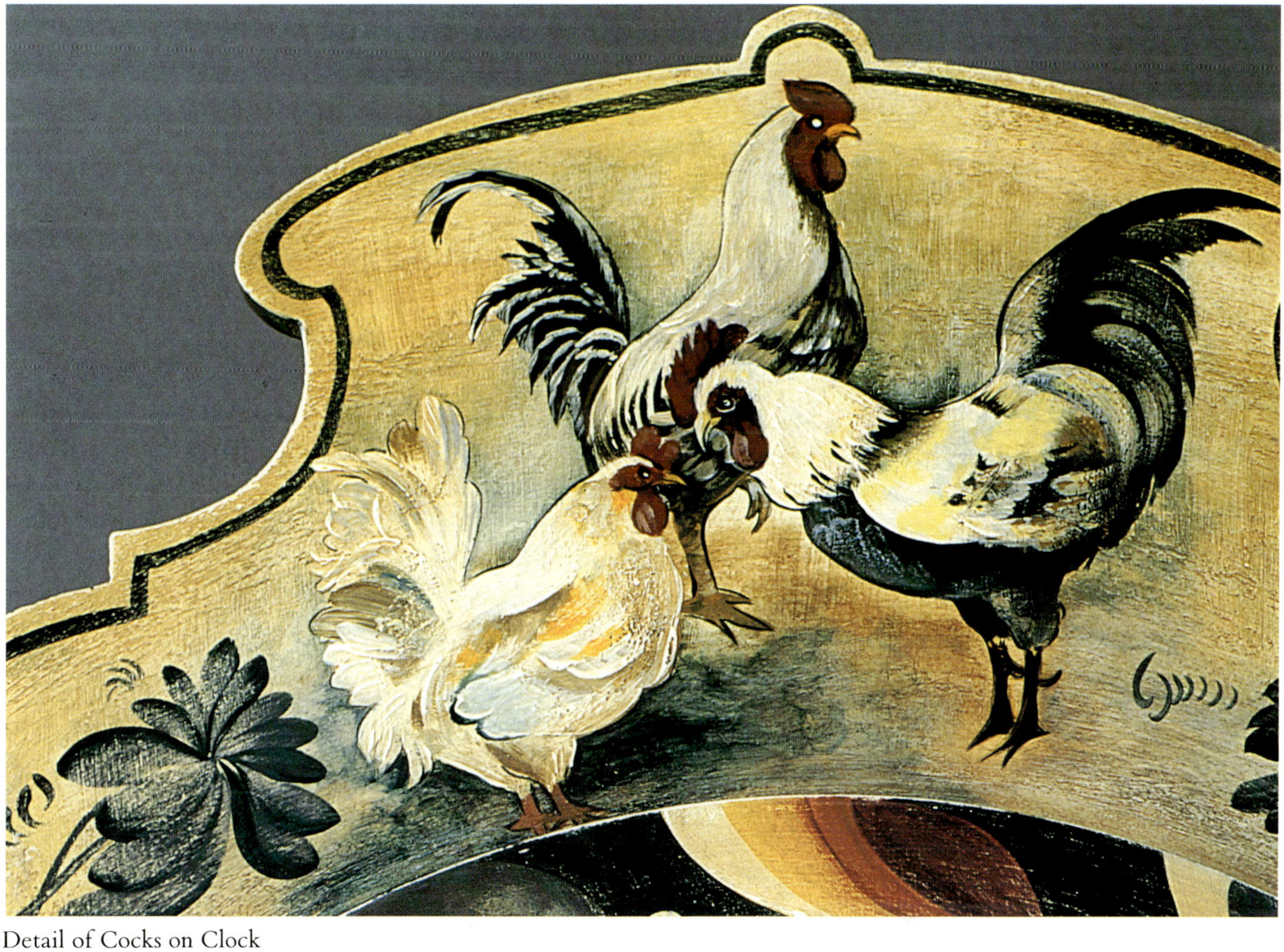

Detail of Cocks on Clock

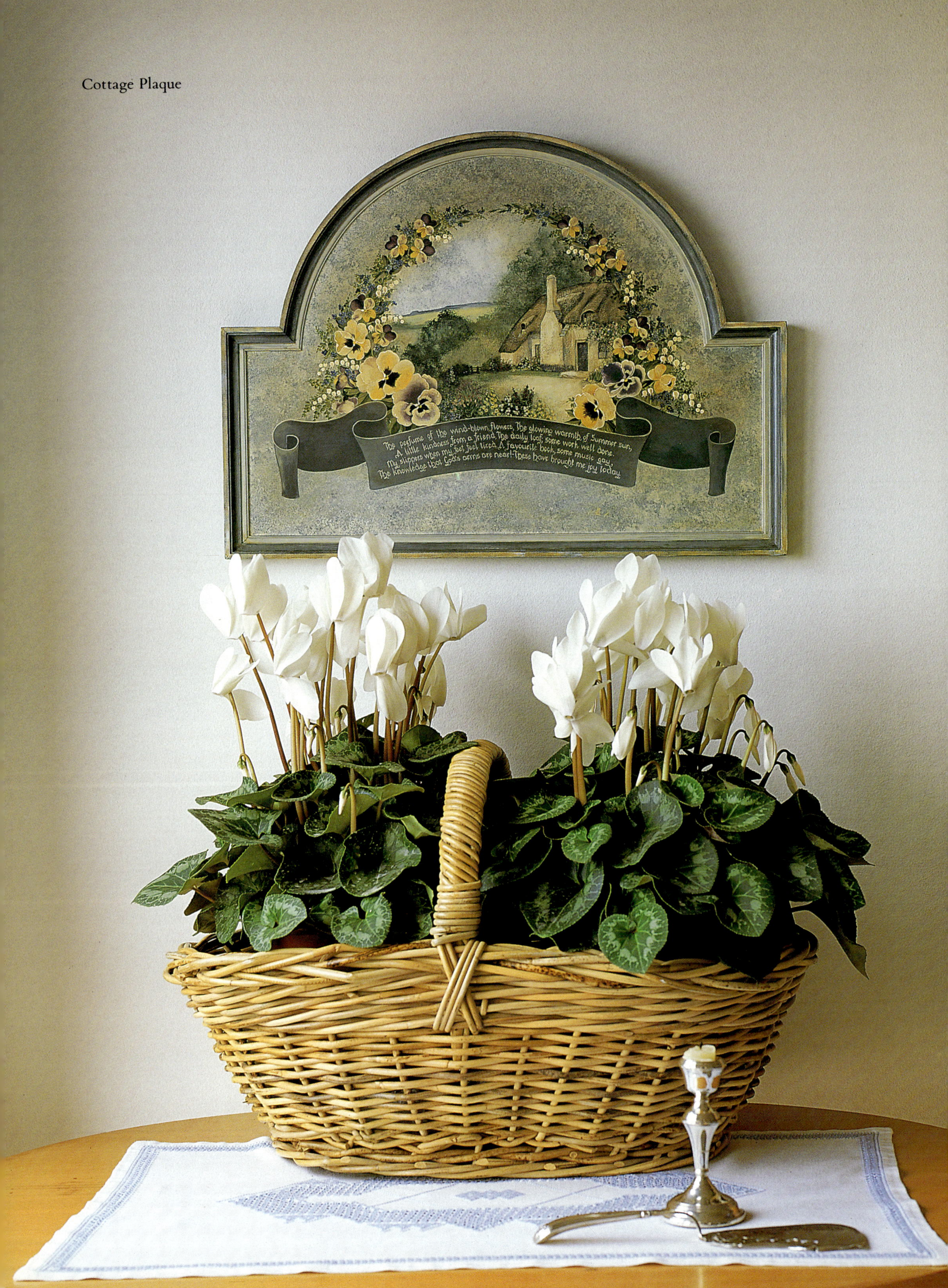

Cottage Plaque

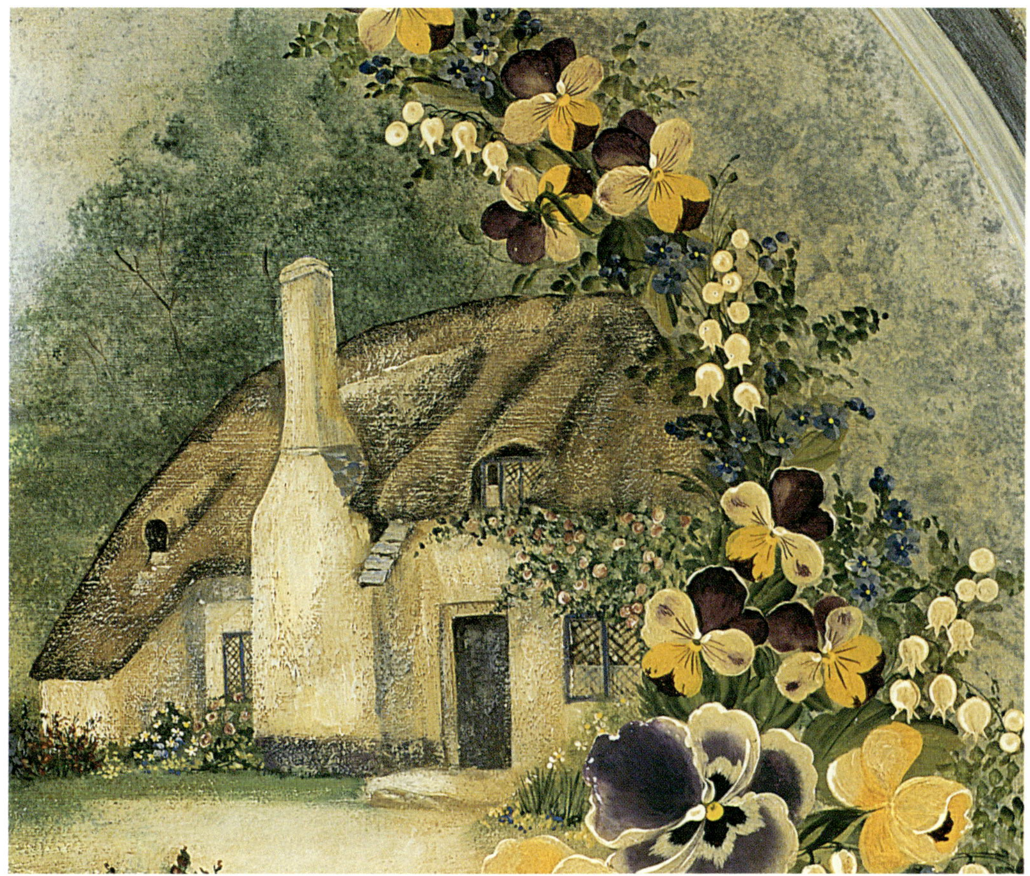

Detail of Cottage on Plaque

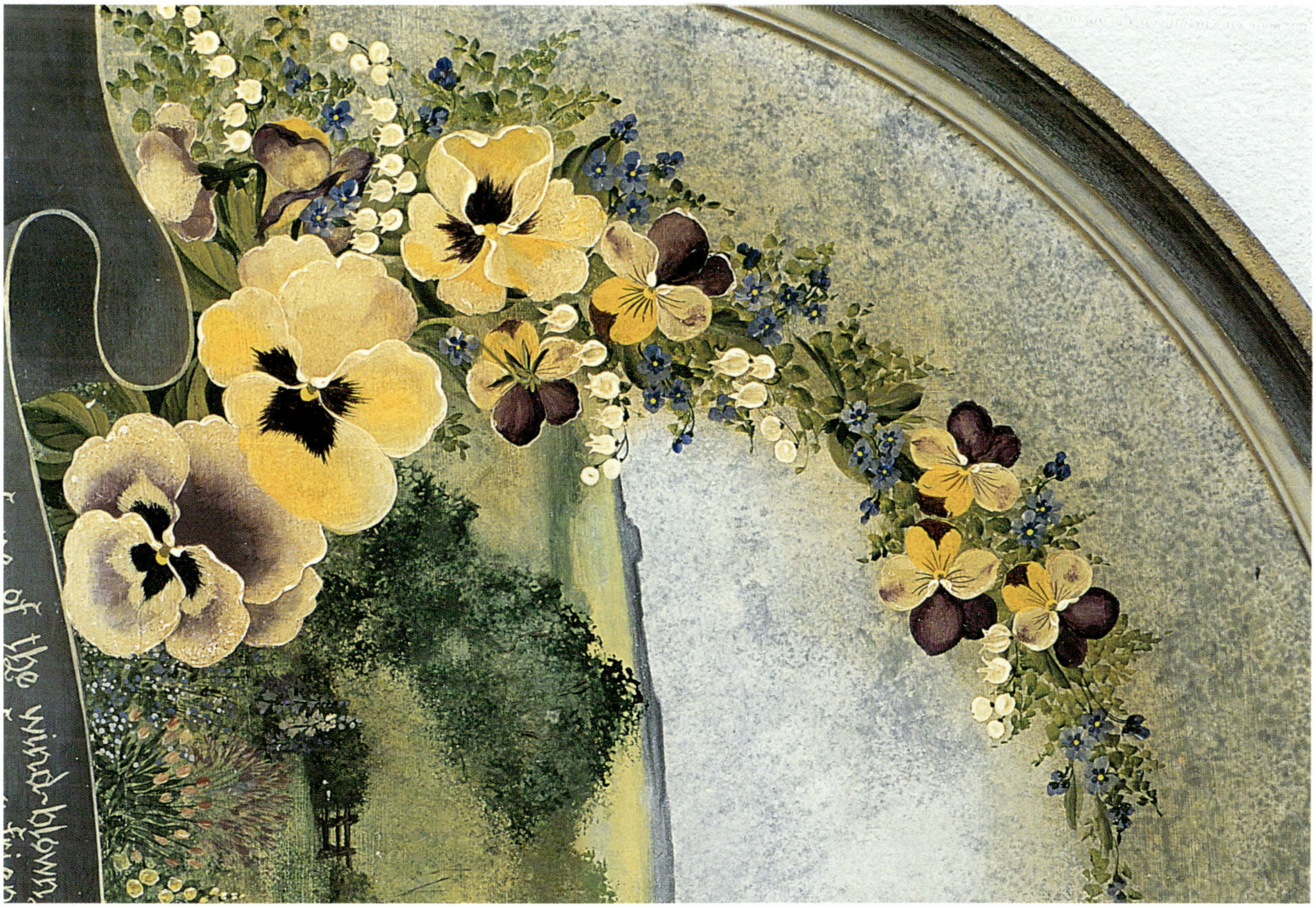

Detail of Garland on Plaque

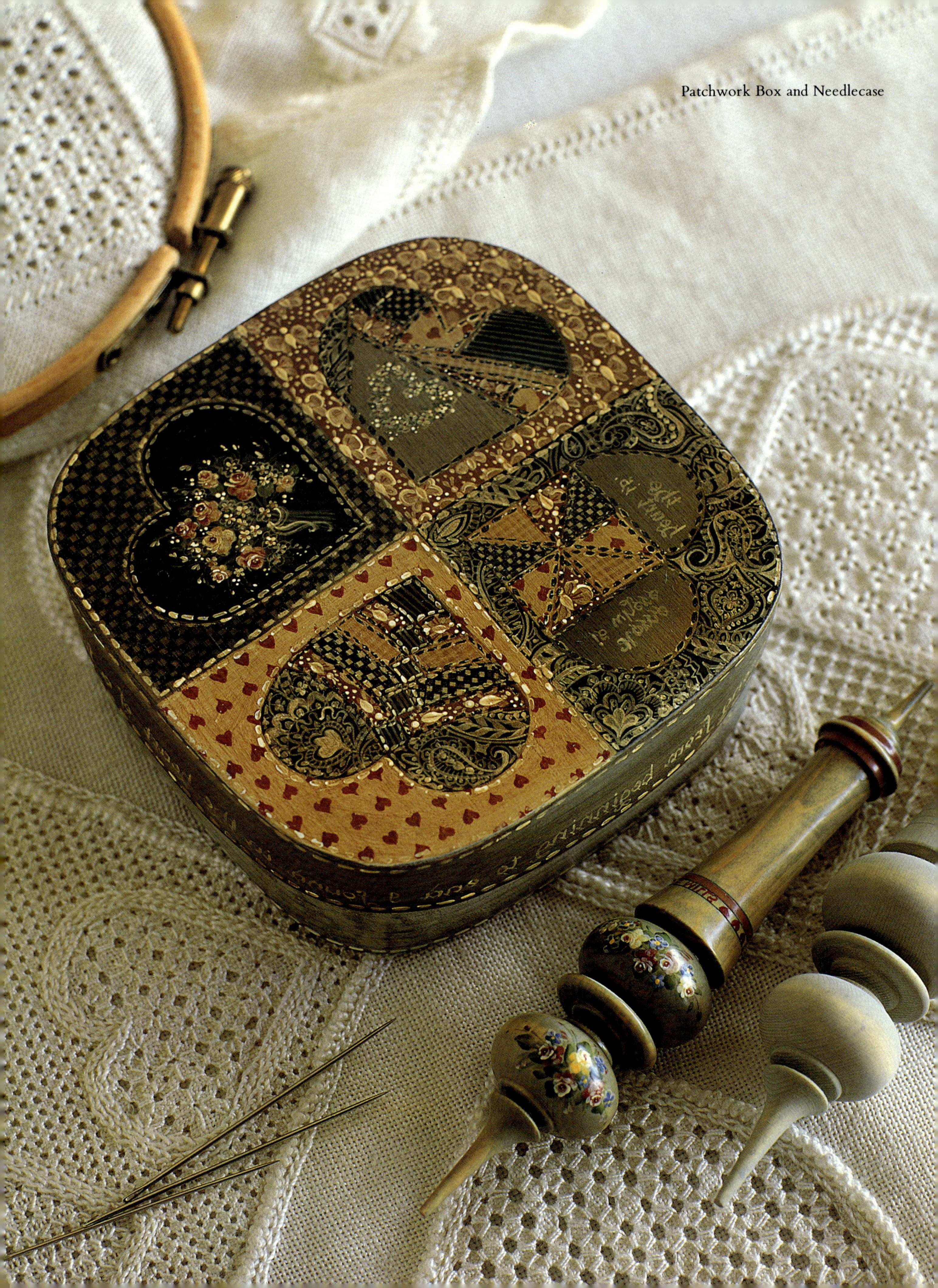

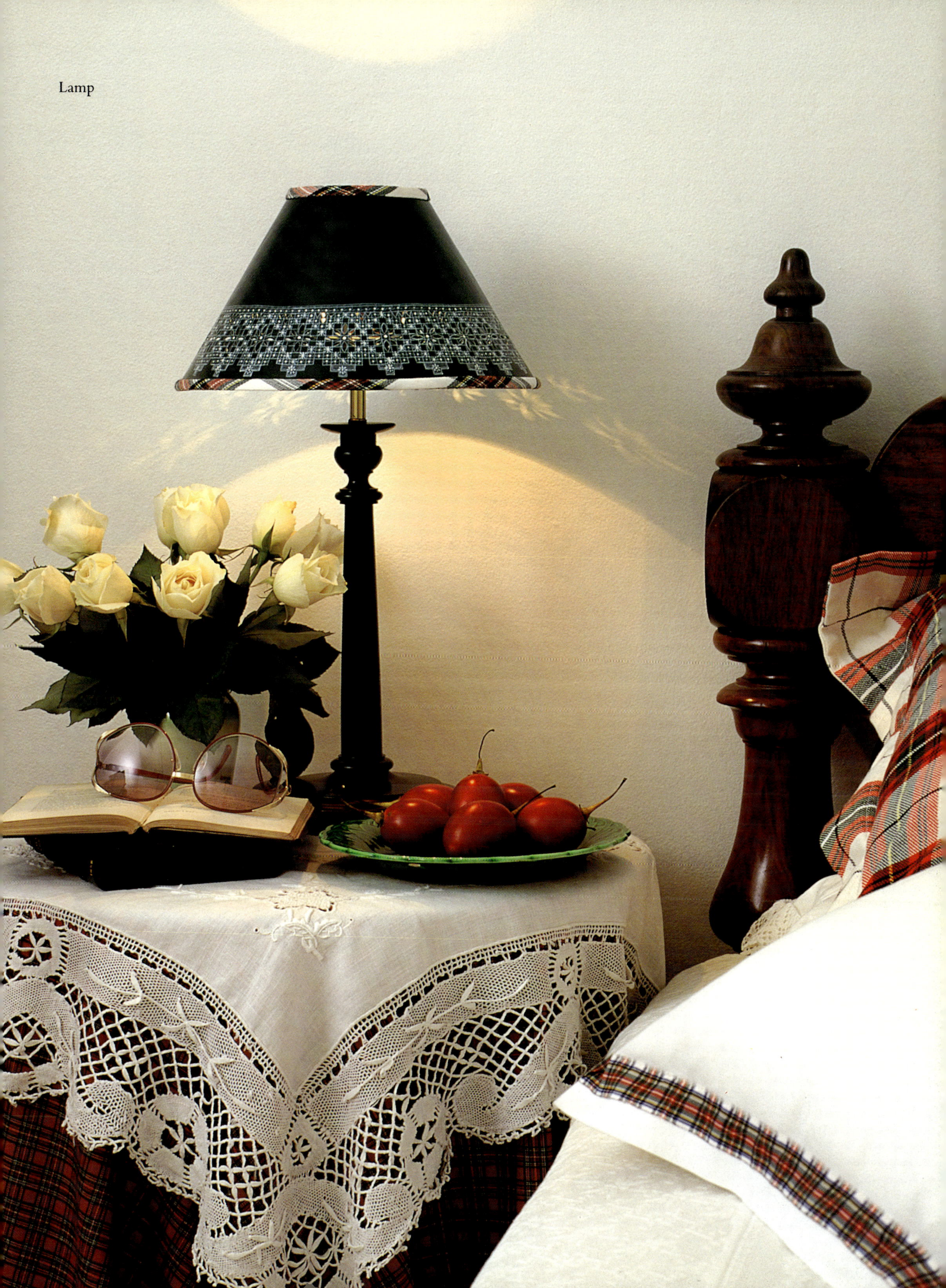

Lamp

Clock

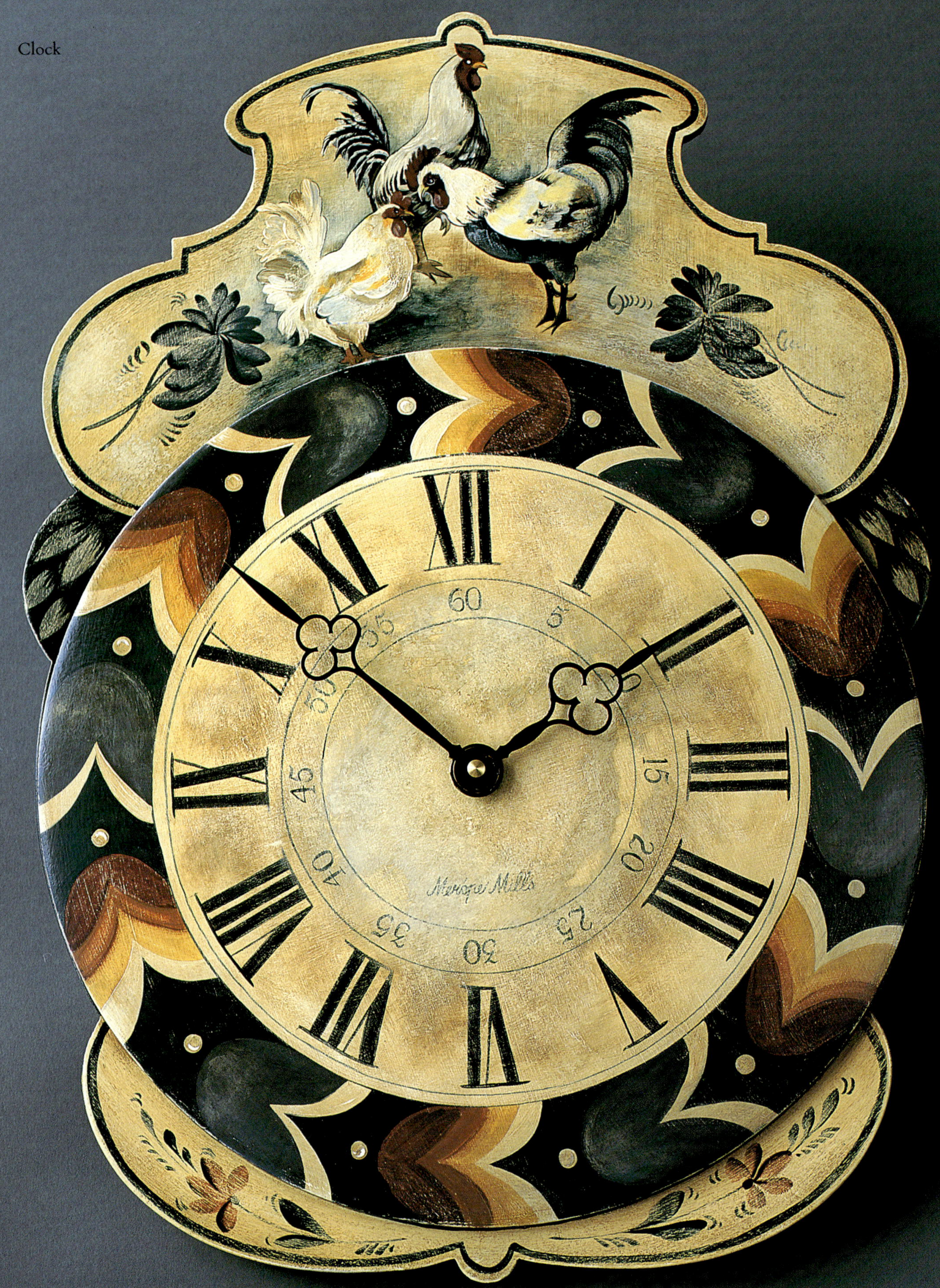

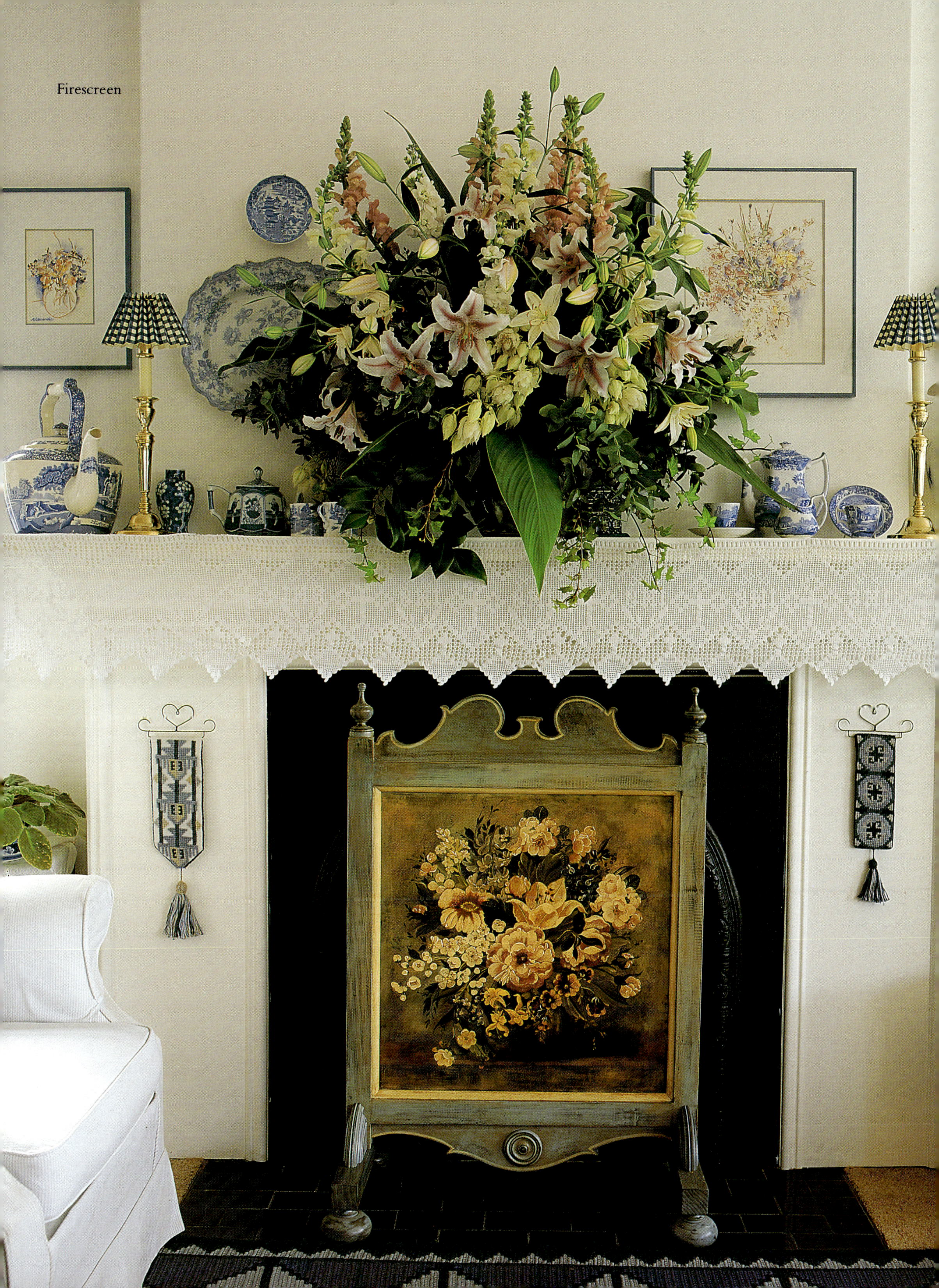

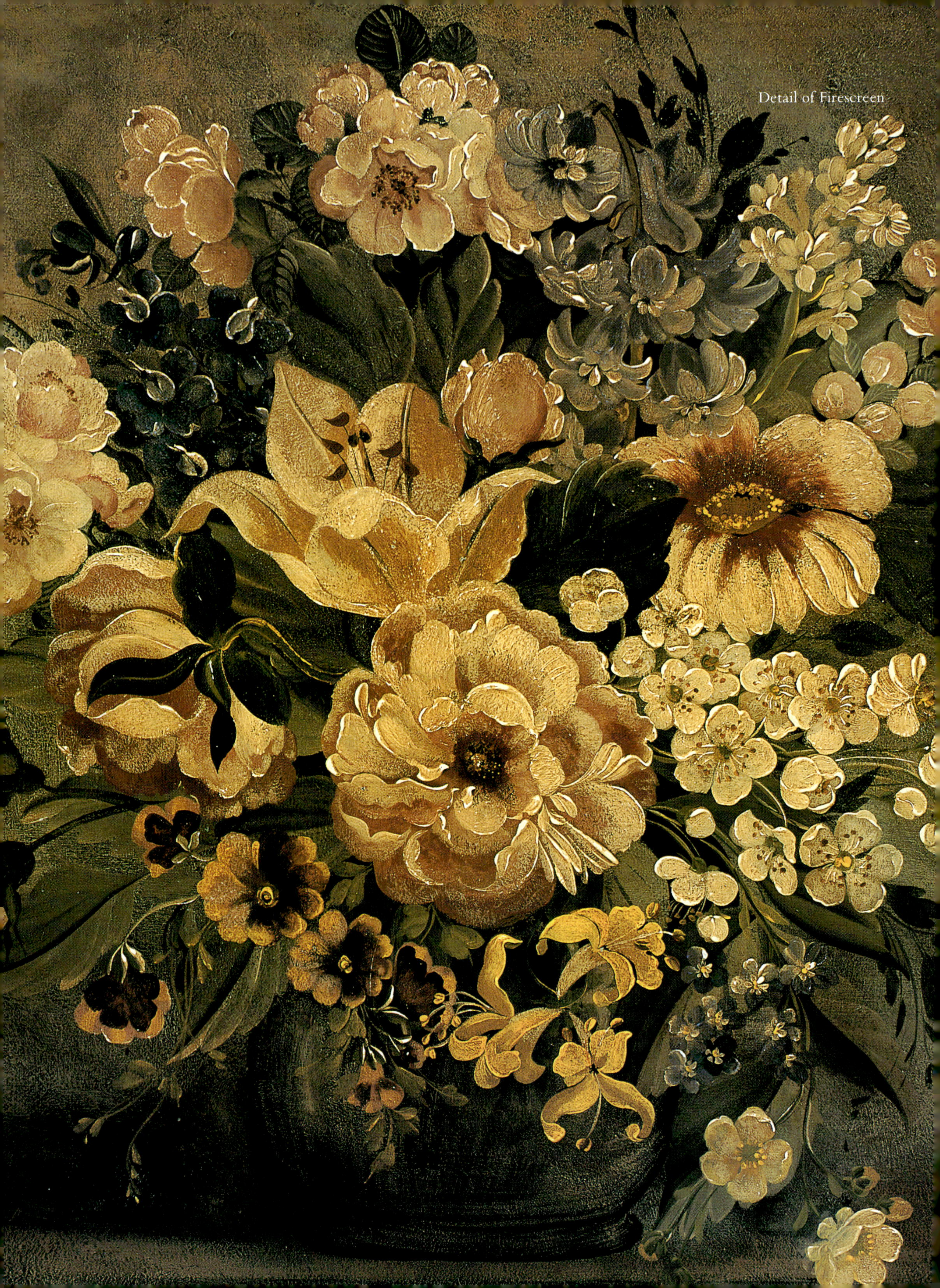
Detail of Firescreen

PATCHWORK BOX

Blessed are the quilters
for they shall be called piecemakers

Requirements:
You will need a square box measuring 10.5 cm (4⅛ inches)
Brushes: Raphael No. 1 (S8404)
Palette: Jo Sonja's — French Blue
Smoked Pearl
Warm White
Fawn
Plum Pink
Yellow Oxide
Matisse — Antique Green or Jo Sonja's Teal Green and Fawn (mixed 1:1)

PREPARATION

Paint the box with one coat of Smoked Pearl. The second coat is a mixture of Warm White and French Blue, making a pale blue.

Sand the box with Wet and Dry Sandpaper and water. Be careful not to lift too much paint off. Wipe clean with a paper towel.

METHOD

- Trace the design onto the lid.
- Paint each section as follows:

a. Paisley:
Mix the French Blue and Warm White together for the background. The pattern is then painted in Warm White.

b. Butterfly:
The background is a mixture of Fawn and Plum Pink. The head and body are painted in thick Warm White.

The wings are painted in a watery Warm White, the marking on the wings in Plum Pink, and the feelers and dots in Warm White.

c. Hearts:
The background is Smoked Pearl. The hearts are painted in a mixture of Plum Pink and Fawn.

d. Check:
The background is painted in a mixture of Fawn and Smoked Pearl. The lines running horizontal and vertical are painted in a watery Warm White.

e. Check blocks:
The background is a mixture of Warm White and French Blue. First paint in the lines and then fill in checker board block in French Blue.

f. Original background colour, that is, the distressed pale blue.

g. Stripes:
The background is French Blue with fine horizontal lines in Warm White.

h. Blue Heart: This is French Blue with a little Smoked Pearl added.

i. Flowers in Blue Heart (h)
Paint in the stems and leaves of the posy in a mixture of Antique Green and Smoked Pearl.

Paint the roses with a base coat of Smoked Pearl.

Some roses are then painted in shades of pink (using Fawn and Plum Pink) and some in a mixture of Fawn and Smoked Pearl.

Highlight the roses with thick Warm White. Refer to the method for the roses on Needlecase (see page 41).

Daisies are Warm White as are the dots and buds. The centres are Yellow Oxide.

A heart of daisies is painted in the crazy patchwork heart. The leaves are Antique Green with Warm White daisies and Plum Pink centres.

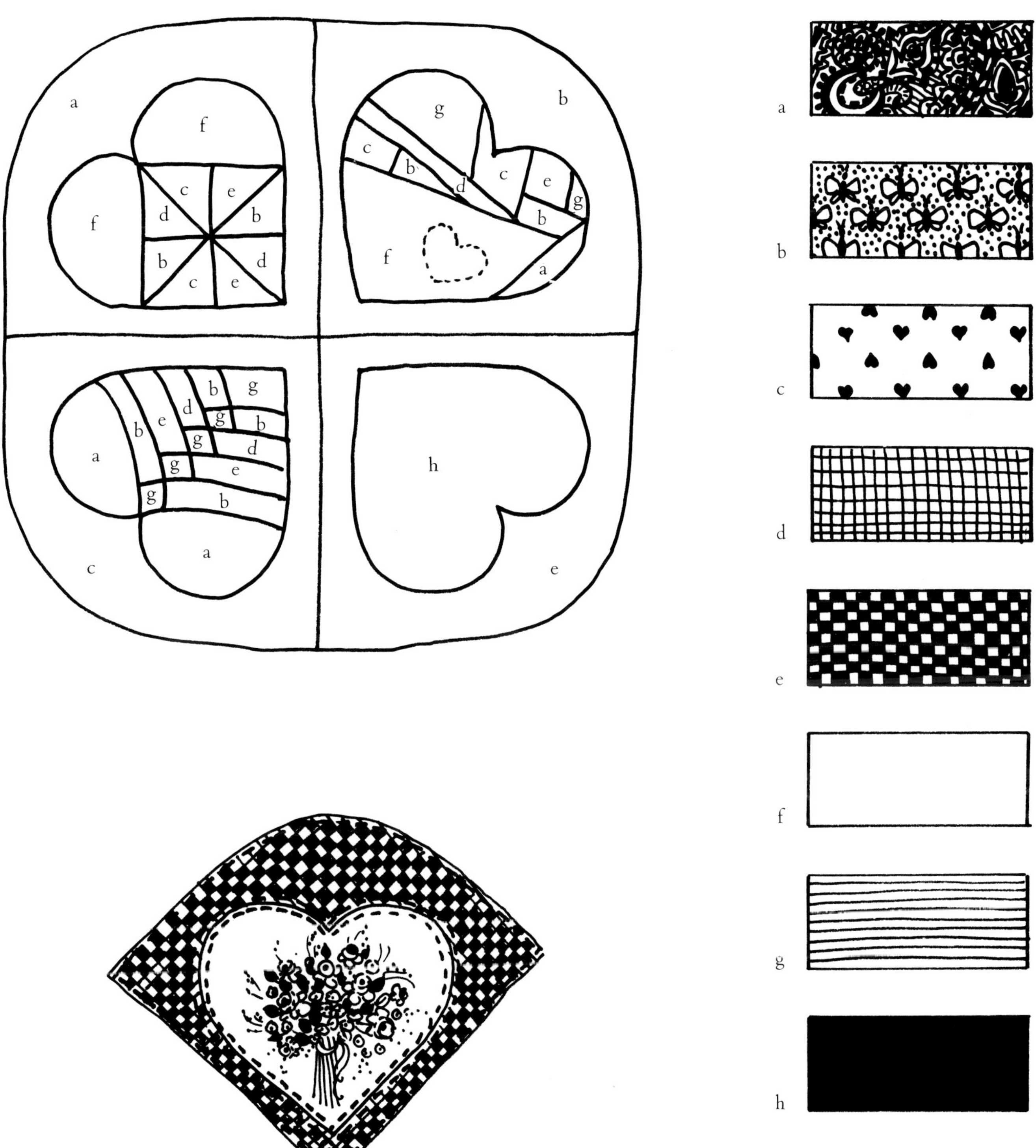
a
b
c
d
e
f
g
h

- The quilting stitches are painted in Warm White around the dark patches and in French Blue where the patches are light. The stitches are also painted in Warm White around the upper and lower edges of the rim of the lid, and the bottom of the box.

  The following verse is painted in Warm White on the rim of the lid:

  And the song from beginning to end
  I found in the heart of a friend.

- Antique.
- Varnish.

LAMP

Let your light so shine before men, that they may see your good works and glorify your Father.

Matthew 5:16

Requirements:
You will need a lampstand 32 cm (12⅝ inches) in height and an electrical fitting, a template shade which measures 10 cm (4 inches) diameter at top, 27.8 cm (11 inches) diameter at bottom and 15.2 cm (6 inches) high
White graphite paper
White chalk pencil
Blu-Strike snap-blade cutter (from newsagent)
Brush: Raphael No. 1
Palette: Jo Sonja's — Warm White
Teal Green
Burgundy
Jo Sonja's All-Purpose Sealer or Matisse Sealer

PREPARATION

A template of the shade can be purchased at a selected lamp shop. You work on this flat. After the shade has been completed you should return it to the shop to be assembled.

Choose a suitable coloured paper from an art shop. I chose a dark green to match our bedroom.

Place template on the coloured paper and trace the outline, then cut it out.

Seal both sides with Matisse or Jo Sonja's Sealer.

As the green was not the exact colour I wanted I gave the shade two coats of Teal Green.

METHOD

- Using a ruler, mark with a chalk pencil 1 cm (½ inch) and then a further 6 cm (2½ inches) from the bottom edge of the shade all the way around to the other end.
- Link up these lines, so forming a border for the lace work.
- Place the tracing on the edge of the border and slip the graphite paper underneath. With a stylus, trace the section of the pattern. The vertical lines can be drawn with a ruler.
- Progressively move the tracing from right to left, tracing each section until the border is complete.
- In watery Warm White paint the vertical and horizontal lines.
- Paint the outlines of large middle flowers and triangles (they are coloured solid black in the design).
- In thick Warm White paint in the stars.
- In watery paint, paint the flower-like fillers, also the fillers in the border on top.
- Paint double lines on top of the border and bottom section of the design.
- Paint a wash in this bottom section and then with thick Warm White, paint the flower.
- Using an eraser remove any graphite lines that are showing.
- Paint in the dots.
- With a snap-blade cutter cut out centre flowers and triangles (black coloured part of design).
- Varnish with three layers of Jo Sonja's or Matisse Clear Sealer, allowing each coat to dry in between. I use a small face sea sponge and drag it from top to bottom of the shade, so working my way to the other end.
- Seal the underside with one coat of sealer.
- Sand the stand and give it two coats of Teal Green.
- Pick out the sections of the stand and paint them in a different colour — I chose Burgundy.
- Varnish.

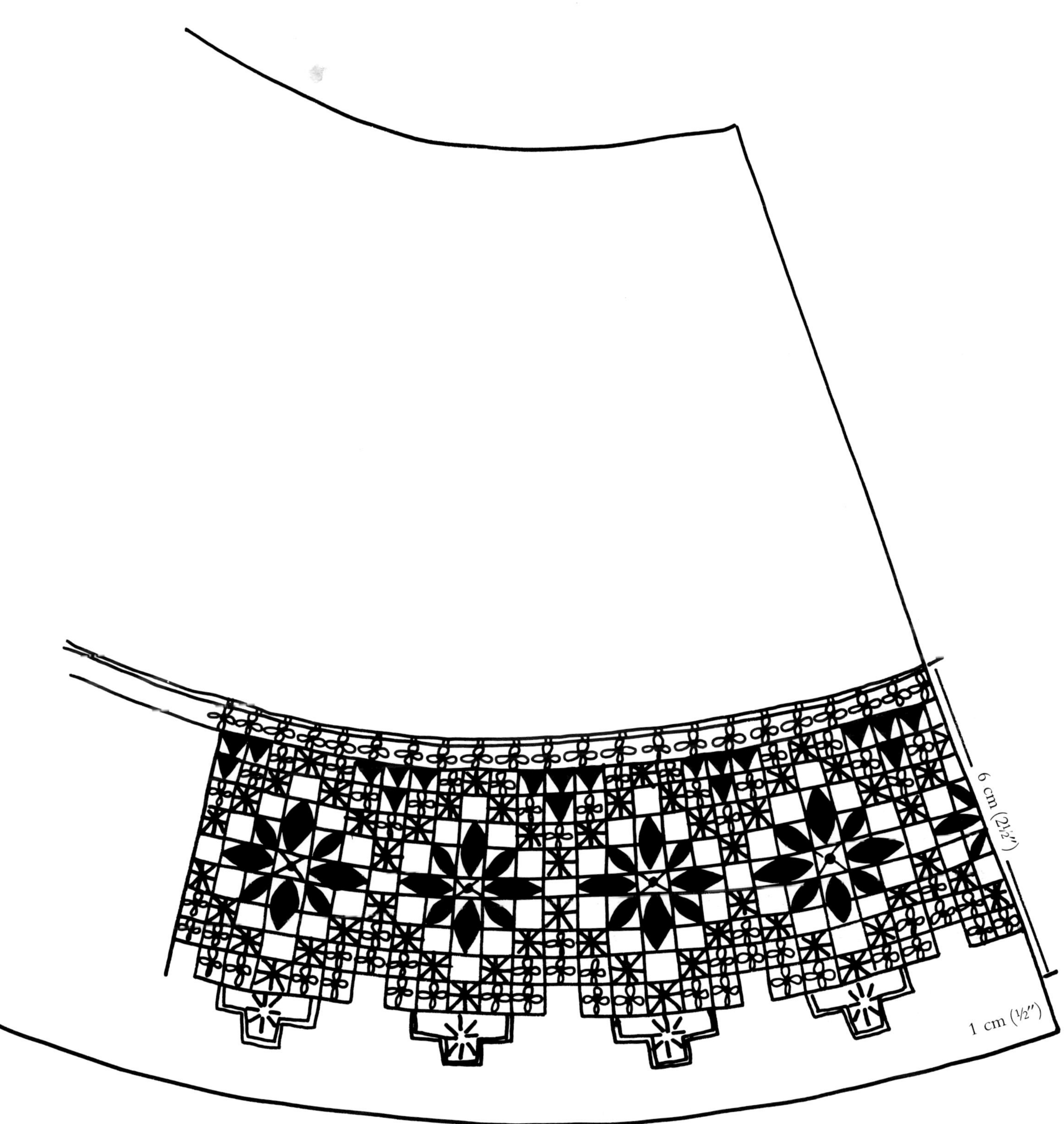
6 cm (2½")
1 cm (½")

Clock

'Oh, be swift to love!
Make haste to be kind.
Do not delay;
the golden moments fly!
Henry W. Longfellow

Requirements:
You will need a clock with a diameter of 31 cm (12 inches)
Brush: Raphael No. 2 or 3
Palette: Jo Sonja's — Smoked Pearl
Warm White
Provincial Beige
Storm Blue
Carbon Black
French Blue
Red Earth
Yellow Oxide
Titanium White

Matisse — Antique White or Jo Sonja's Warm White
Burgundy or Jo Sonja's Burgundy plus Carbon Black (mixed 10:1)

PREPARATION

Paint clock in Smoked Pearl. Give it a second coat.

Using thick Warm White and the Dry Brush Method add texture to the top of the clock and the dial.

METHOD

- Stick a piece of thick plastic over the centre hole of the clock with masking tape. This will enable you to put your compass point in the middle and draw in the four circles.
- Trace the design of the pattern which surrounds the face.

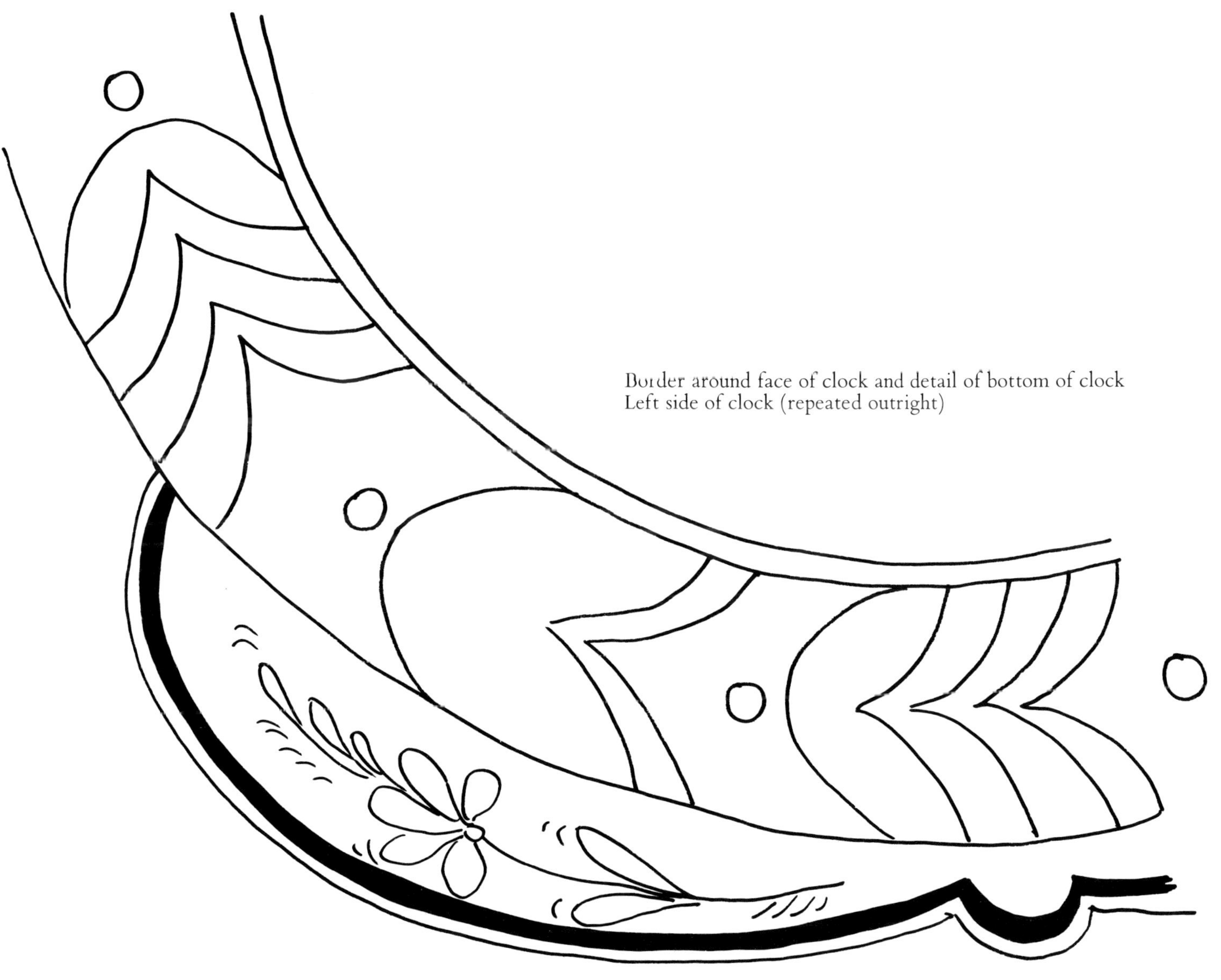

Border around face of clock and detail of bottom of clock
Left side of clock (repeated outright)

- Paint in four circles in Storm Blue.
- Paint between the tulip shapes of the design with a mixture of Storm Blue and Carbon Black.
- The base of the dark tulips is French Blue. The top of the dark tulip is Antique White, as is the dot between the tulips.
- The base of the coloured tulip is a mixture of Red Earth and Burgundy. The second section is a mixture of Red Earth and Burgundy and Yellow Oxide. The third section is painted in Yellow Oxide. The fourth section is Antique White.
- Extra texture is added to the dial with a touch of Provincial Beige. The numbers are painted in a mixture of Storm Blue and Carbon Blue.
- The circles and minute numbers are painted in Storm Blue.
- Top of Clock:

Rooster (1):

Chest: The background is a mixture of Provincial Beige and Black. With the Dry Brush Method add Titanium White feathers and Provincial Beige feathers.

Back: The back of the rooster is Titanium White. Add thick Titanium White to imitate feathers.

Tail: The tail is a mixture of Provincial Beige and Black with a highlight of Titanium White mixed with Provincial Beige.

Feet: Provincial Beige outlined with Black.

Bill: Yellow Oxide.

Comb: A mixture of Red Earth and Burgundy, highlighted with Red Earth.

Eye: Black with a White dot.

Cock (2):

Chest and Tail: These are painted in a mixture of Storm Blue and Black.

Highlight the front of the chest with White using the Dry Brush Method and imitate the feathers of the tail in the same colour and method.

Back: The back is painted in White with shadings of Provincial Beige, a mixture of Storm Blue and Black and a mixture of Yellow Oxide and White.

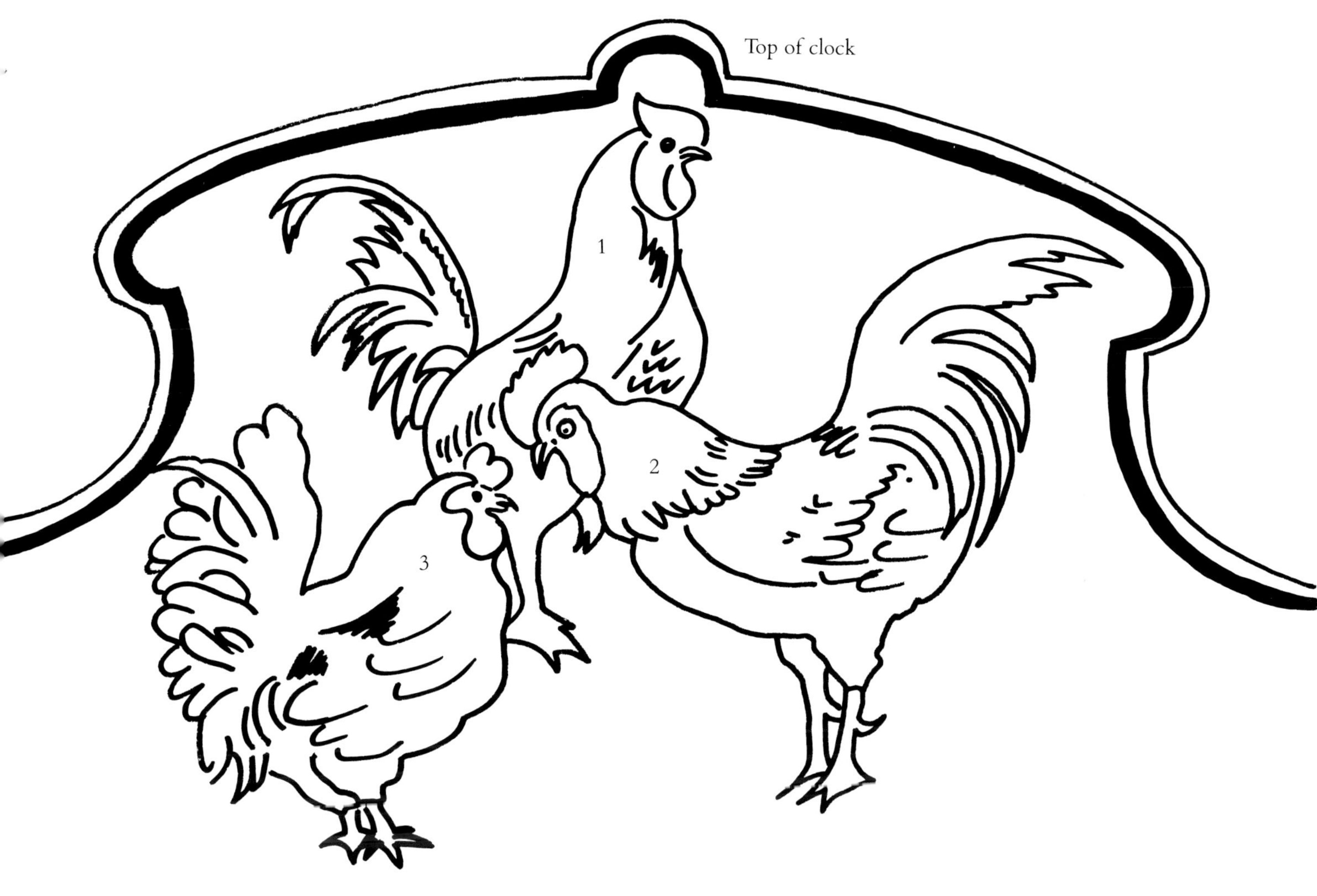

The feathers around the head are thick White.

Bill: Yellow Oxide.

Comb: A mixture of Red Earth and Burgundy.

Eye: Black with White dot.

Feet: A mixture of Provincial Beige and Black.

Cockerel (3):

This is an untidy feathered bird. The bird is painted in White, then the feathers are painted in thick White, Provincial Beige, a touch of Storm Blue with the addition of a little Yellow Oxide (refer to photograph).

Feet: Red Earth.

Bill: Yellow Oxide.

Comb: A mixture of Burgundy and Red Earth.

Eye: Black with a White dot.

Outline the birds in Black and shade in a little Storm Blue around the edge.

The flowers on either side of the birds are painted in Storm Blue with comma strokes.

Below the flowers, paint the background a mixture of Storm Blue and Black and the leaf design in a mixture of Smoked Pearl with a touch of Storm Blue.

- The daisy at the bottom of the clock is a mixture of Red Earth and Burgundy and a comma stroke forms the daisy. The leaves and stem and commas are all in Storm Blue.

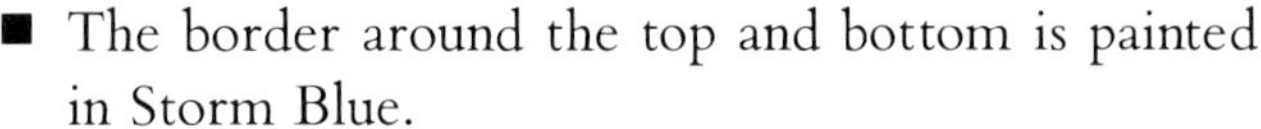

- The border around the top and bottom is painted in Storm Blue.
- Antique.
- Varnish.

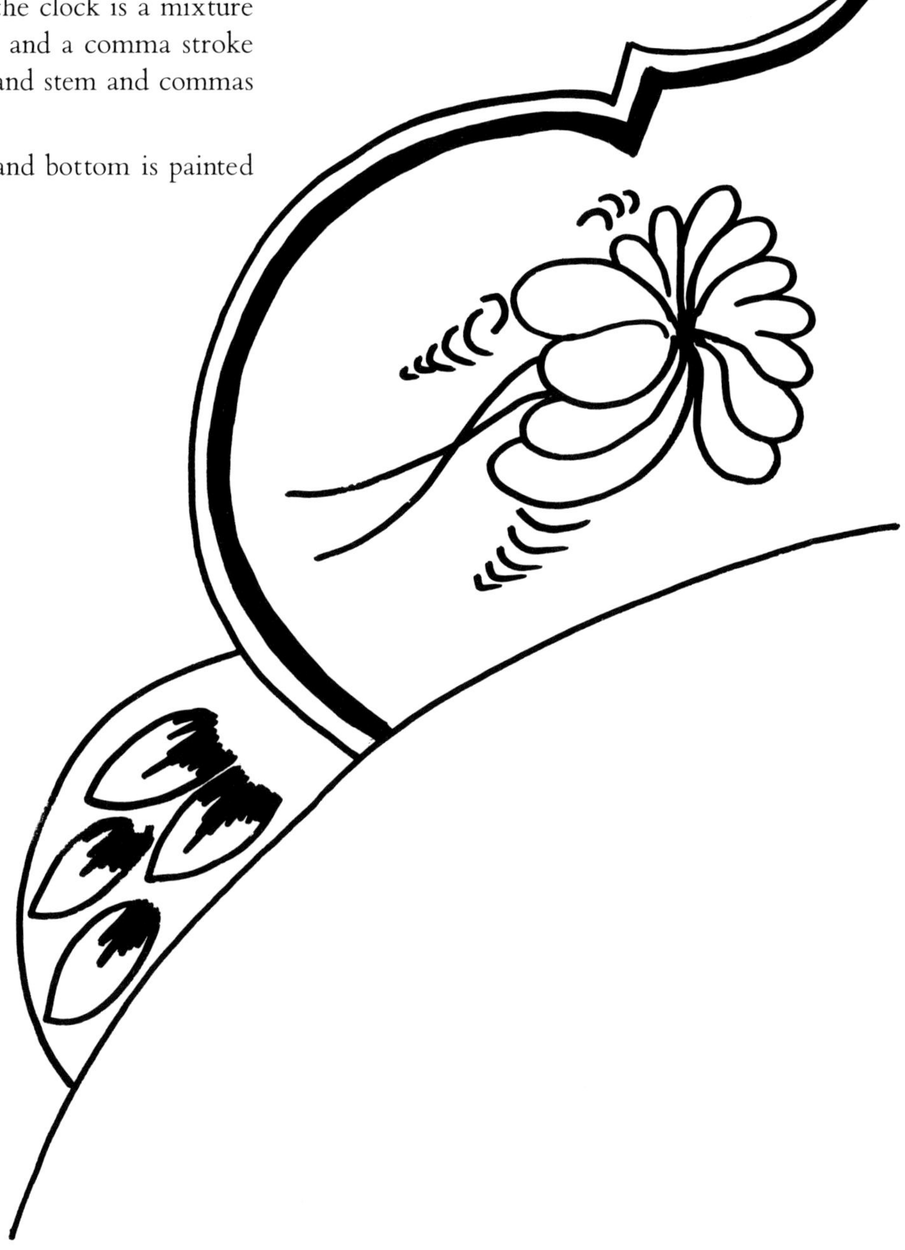

FIRESCREEN

We cannot kindle when we will
The fire that in the heart resides,
The spirit bloweth and it still,
In mystery our soul abides.

Matthew Arnold

Requirements:
You will need a firescreen, 54.5 cm x 52 cm (20½ inches x 21½ inches) within a frame
Brushes: Raphael No. 3 and No. 5
Palette: Jo Sonja's — Teal Green
Carbon Black
French Blue
Smoked Pearl
Green Oxide
Fawn
Plum Pink
Red Earth
Raw Umber
Raw Sienna
Yellow Oxide
Burgundy
Warm White
Yellow Light
Burnt Sienna
Sapphire Blue
Prussian Blue
Moss Green
Cadmium Yellow Mid

Matisse — Antique Green or Jo Sonja's Teal Green plus Fawn (mixed 1:1)
Antique White or Jo Sonja's Warm White

PREPARATION

Apply a mixture of Teal Green, Carbon Black and French Blue.

With the Dry Brush Method add a mixture of Antique Green and Smoked Pearl.

METHOD

- Trace design on the screen.
- Dark shade around the left side of vase, also along the bottom of the vase, running along the width (as if the vase is sitting on a table).
- Add a mixture of Red Earth and Smoked Pearl to the table.
- Paint the leaves as they are painted in the Iron Pot (page 43).
- Paint the light side of the leaves in a mixture of Green Oxide and Smoked Pearl.
- Paint the dark side of leaves in Green Oxide with a sideload of Teal Green.
- You will need to trace the flowers and vase on again as the leaves form the background.
- Paint the vase in a mixture of Teal Green and Carbon Black, and using the Dry Brush Method add Smoked Pearl.
- FLOWERS:

Give two coats of Smoked Pearl to all the flowers.

a. Centre Rose: Use a No. 5 Raphael brush
   Paint the rose in a mixture of Plum Pink, Red Earth and Fawn. Trace in the detail of the petals. With thick Antique White, and using the Dry Brush Method, edge each petal, pulling the paint down into the base colour. Blend a centre of Burgundy, then add Raw Sienna plus Yellow Oxide dots. Add White dots.

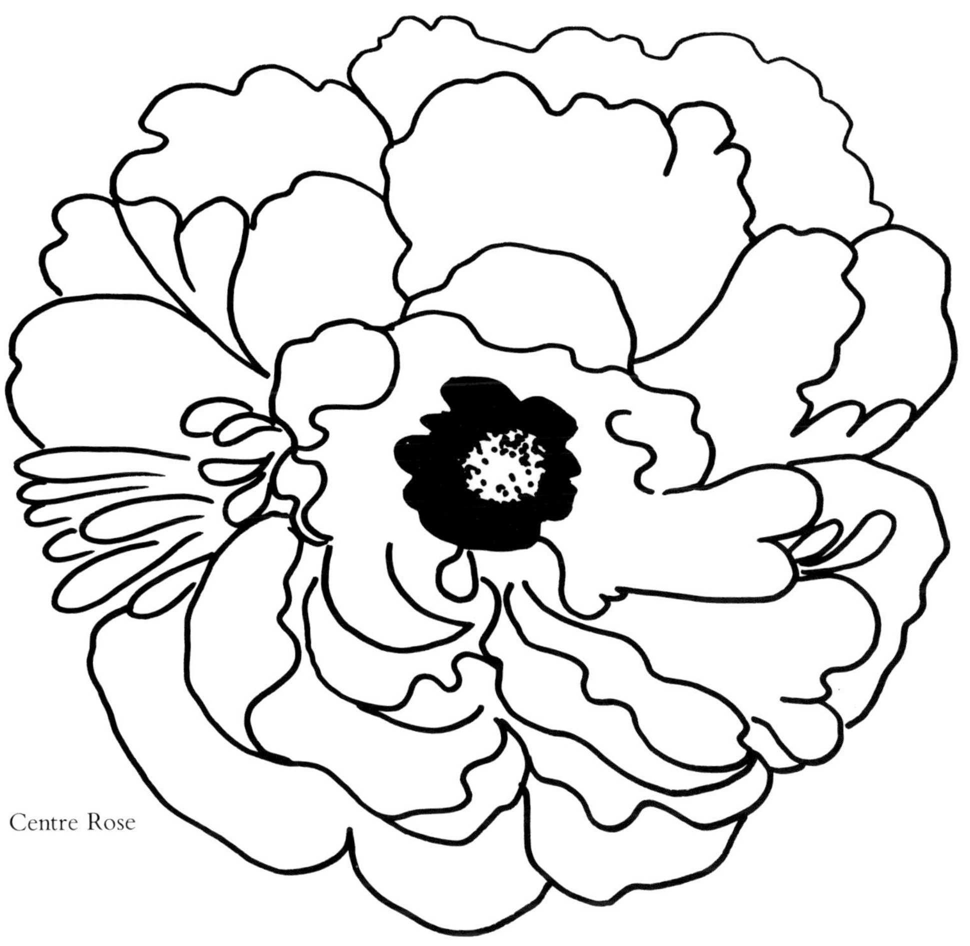

Centre Rose

b. Side Rose: Use a Raphael No. 5 brush
The outer petals are painted in a mixture of Burgundy, Plum Pink and Red Earth. Once they are dry add a mixture of Fawn and Red Earth using the Dry Brush Method.

The inner petals are a mixture of Plum Pink and Fawn. Using Antique White pull the paint down from the outer edge of the petal.

The calyx and stem are Teal Green with a highlight of Cadmium Yellow Mid.

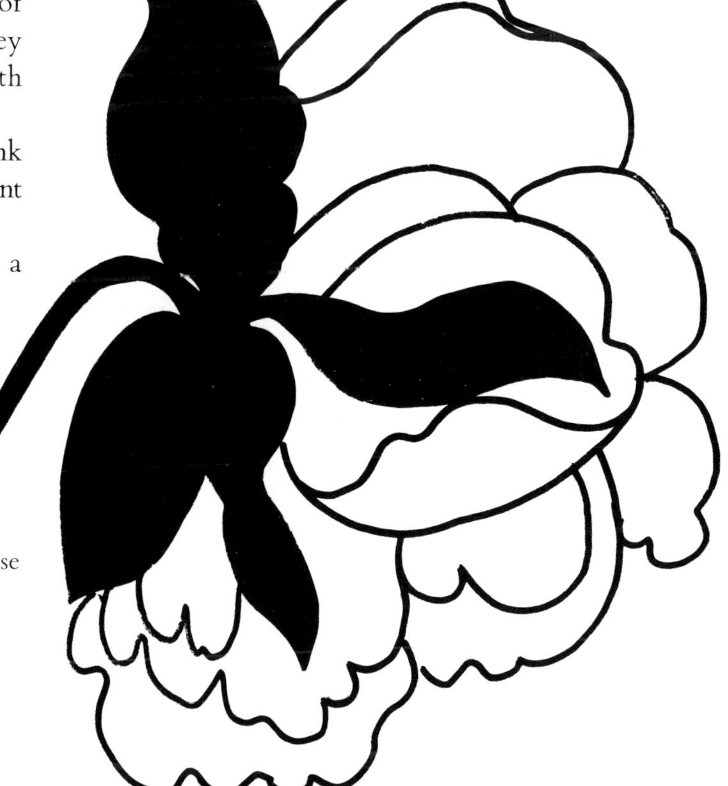

Side Rose

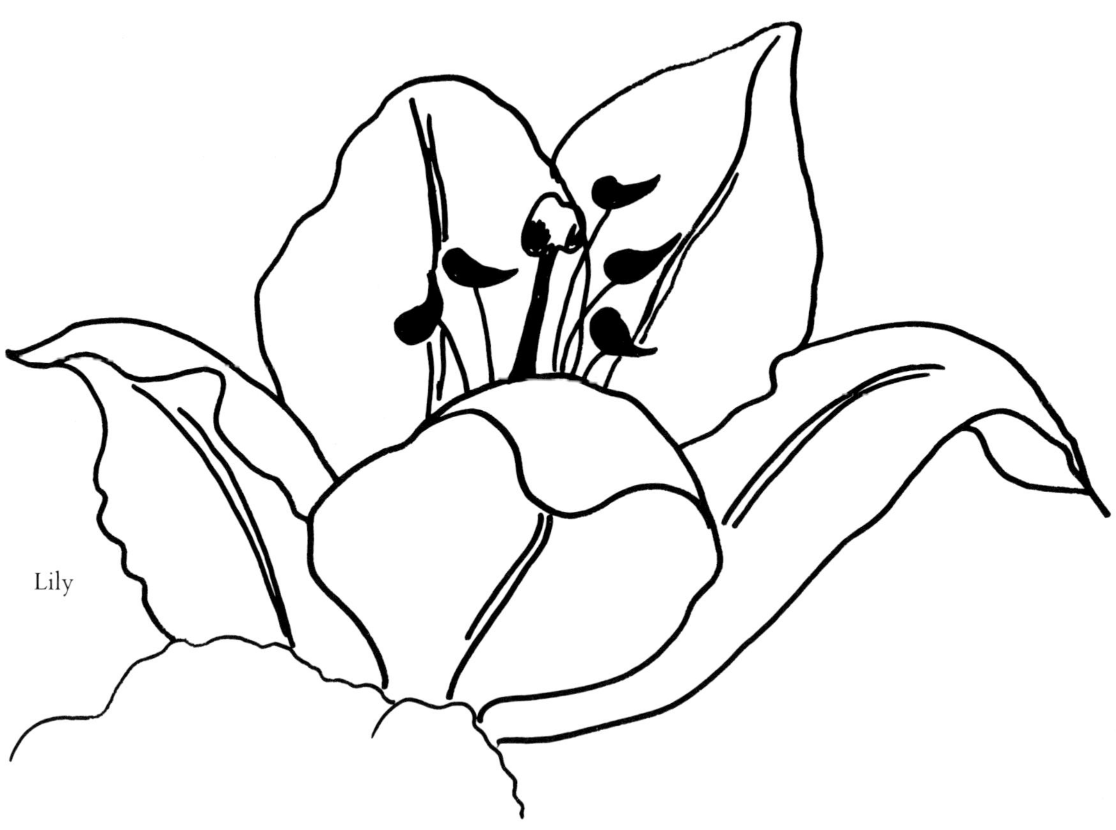

Lily

c. Lily: Use a Raphael No. 5 brush
Paint the lily in a mixture of Warm White and Yellow Oxide. Highlight the petals with Warm White and shade with Yellow Oxide. Paint the middle vein in White and a Raw Umber line on the one side.

Pistil: Paint the pistil in Yellow Oxide and shade with Raw Umber.

Stamens: Paint the stem in Raw Umber, with the pollen sac in Burnt Sienna.

d. Daisy: Use a Raphael No. 5 brush
Paint the daisy in Red Earth. Pull Antique White from the outer edges of top petals using the Dry Brush Method. Bring in thick White commas from bottom petals in towards centre.

Paint an egg-shape of Raw Sienna in the middle. Add Cadmium Yellow Mid dots around the egg-shape.

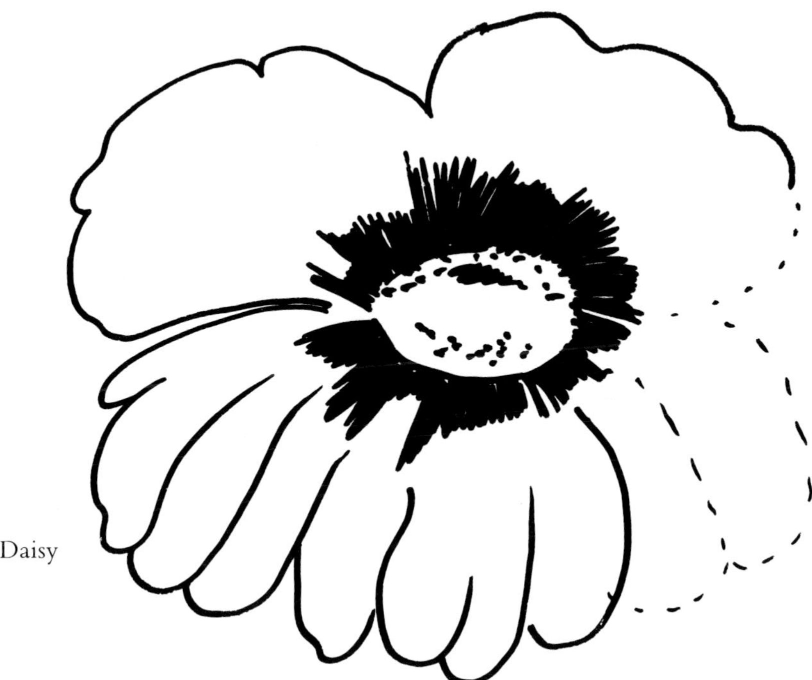
Daisy

e. Polyanthus Primrose: Use a Raphael No. 3 brush With a mixture of Burgundy and Fawn and Warm White, paint the right side of the open flowers and outer petals of side flowers.

With a mixture of Burgundy and Carbon Black, paint around the centre and left side of the open flowers and inner petals of the side flowers.

Mix Cadmium Yellow Mid and Warm White together and add touches to all the petals.

The calyx and stem are painted in Green Oxide with a sideload of Warm White.

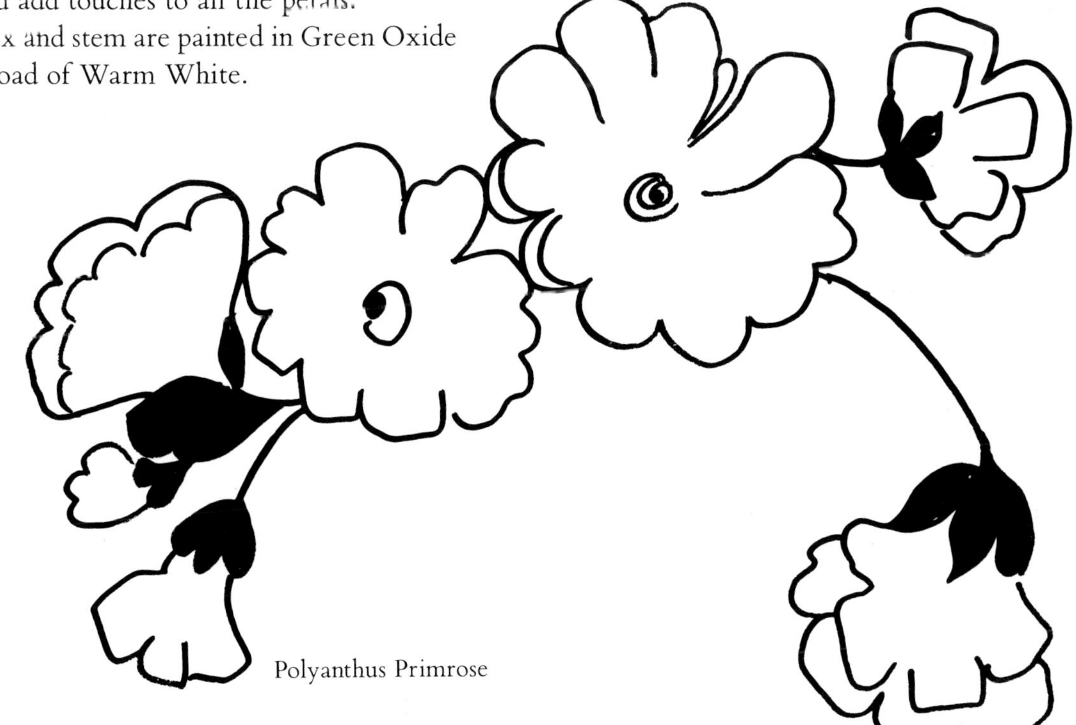
Polyanthus Primrose

f. Freesias: Use a Raphael No. 3 brush
Paint the freesias in Yellow Oxide.

The base of the flowers is a mixture of Warm White and Yellow Oxide.

With thick Cadmium Yellow Mid highlight the petals as they turn and twist (see photograph in the colour section).

The stems of the stamens are painted in Warm White while the pollen is painted with Burnt Sienna and a Cadmium Yellow Mid highlight.

g. Windflowers: Use a Raphael No. 3 brush
Paint flowers in Smoked Pearl with a touch of Carbon Black. Add thick Warm White to the edges of the petals as shown in the Step-By-Step Windflowers of Sewing Box (see colour section).

Paint stems in a mixture of Green Oxide and Yellow Light and sideload with Warm White. Calyxes are painted in a mixture of Yellow Light and Teal Green.

The centres of the flowers are Oxide Green with Yellow Light.

The stamen stems are thick Warm White with Burnt Sienna dots.

Freesias

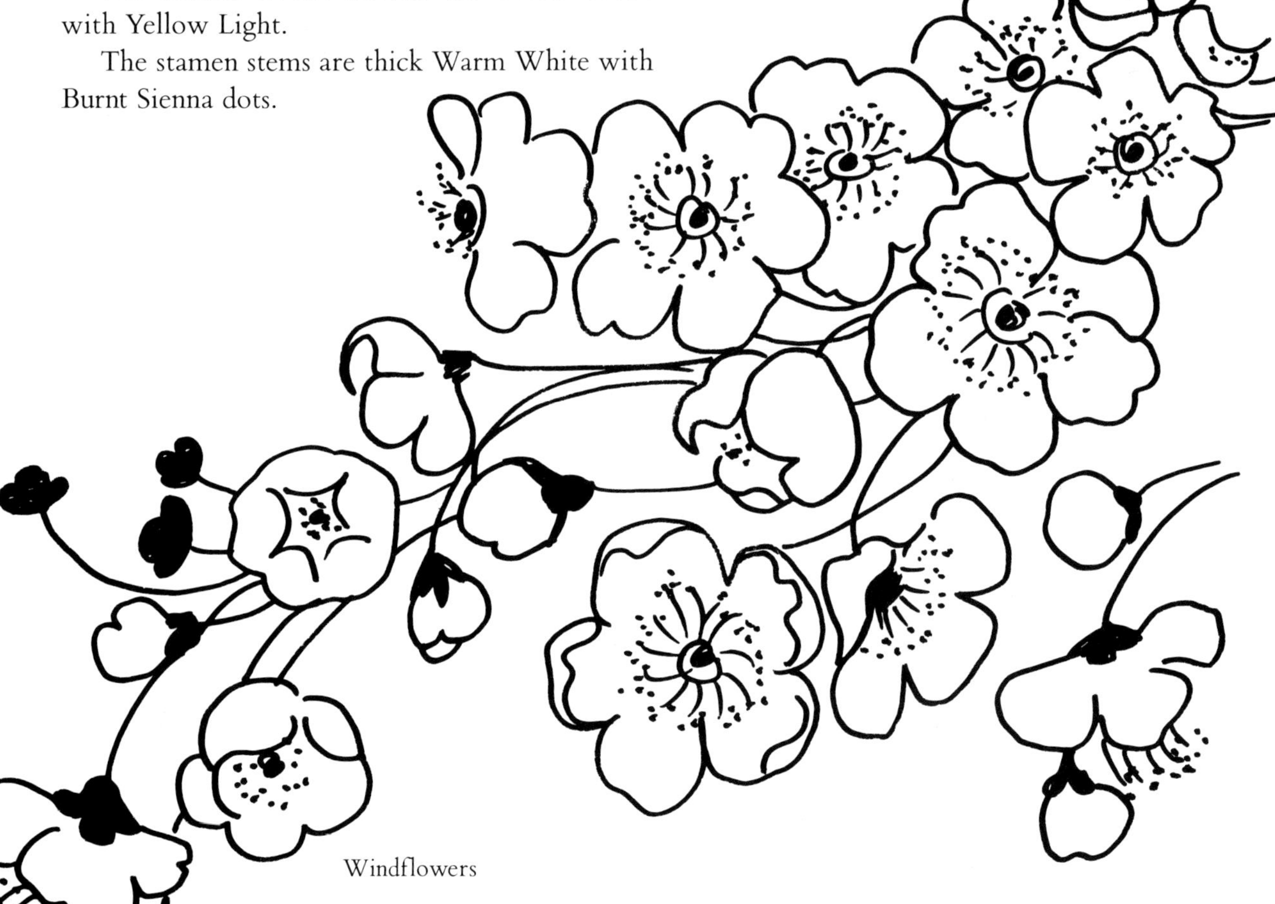

Windflowers

h. Delphiniums (Pale Blue): Use a Raphael No. 3 brush
Paint the flowers in a mixture of Antique Green and Sapphire Blue.

Paint the stems in a mixture of Green Oxide and Yellow Oxide. Add Warm White to Blue mixture so making a pale blue. Load your brush in this pale blue and pick up a sideload of Warm White. Paint in individual petals.

Add Warm White commas in centre so making it a double Delphinium. Shade sections with a mixture of French Blue and Sapphire Blue.

i. Delphiniums (Dark Blue): Use a Raphael No. 3 brush
The petals are painted in Ultramarine Blue.

The deep shading towards the centre is in Prussian Blue.

Highlight the outer edge of the petals in Warm White and paint the centre in a paler blue mixture of Sapphire Blue and Warm White with Warm White highlights.

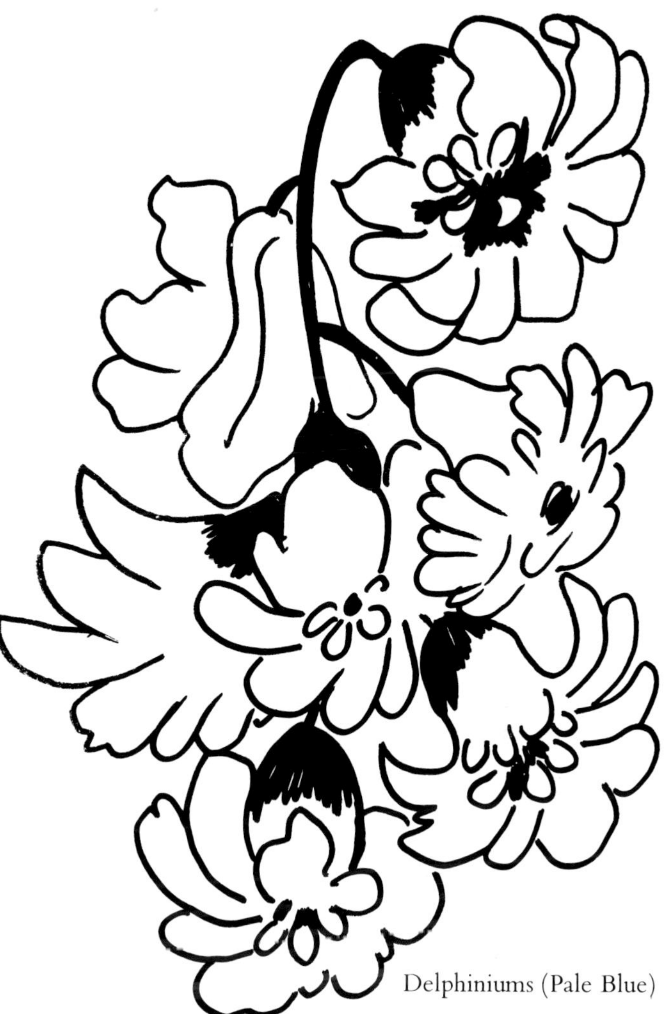

Delphiniums (Pale Blue)

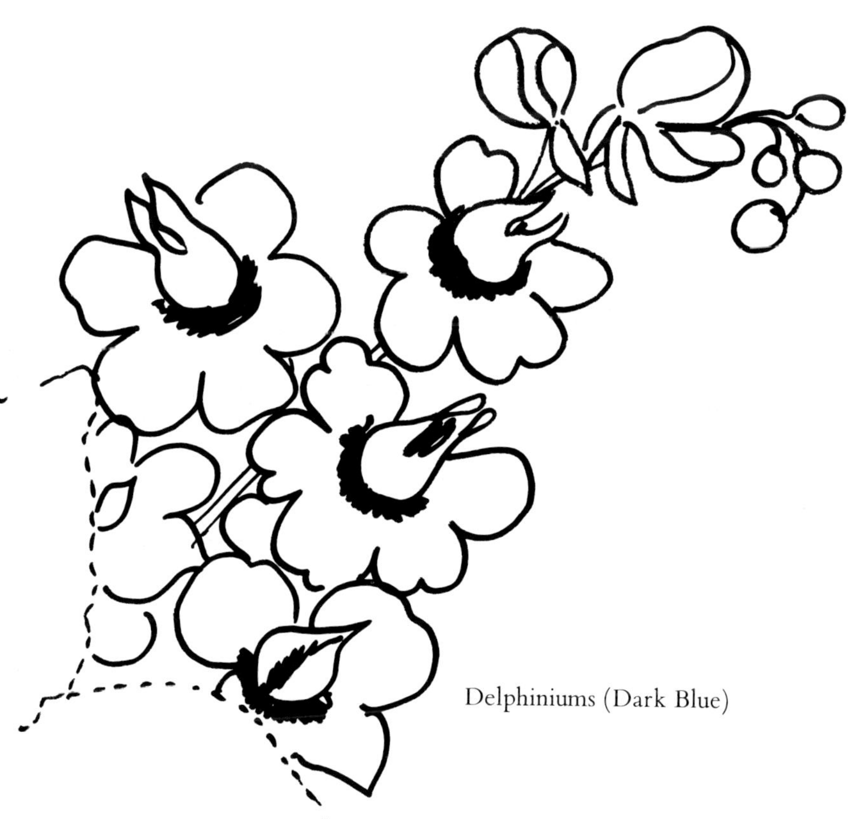

Delphiniums (Dark Blue)

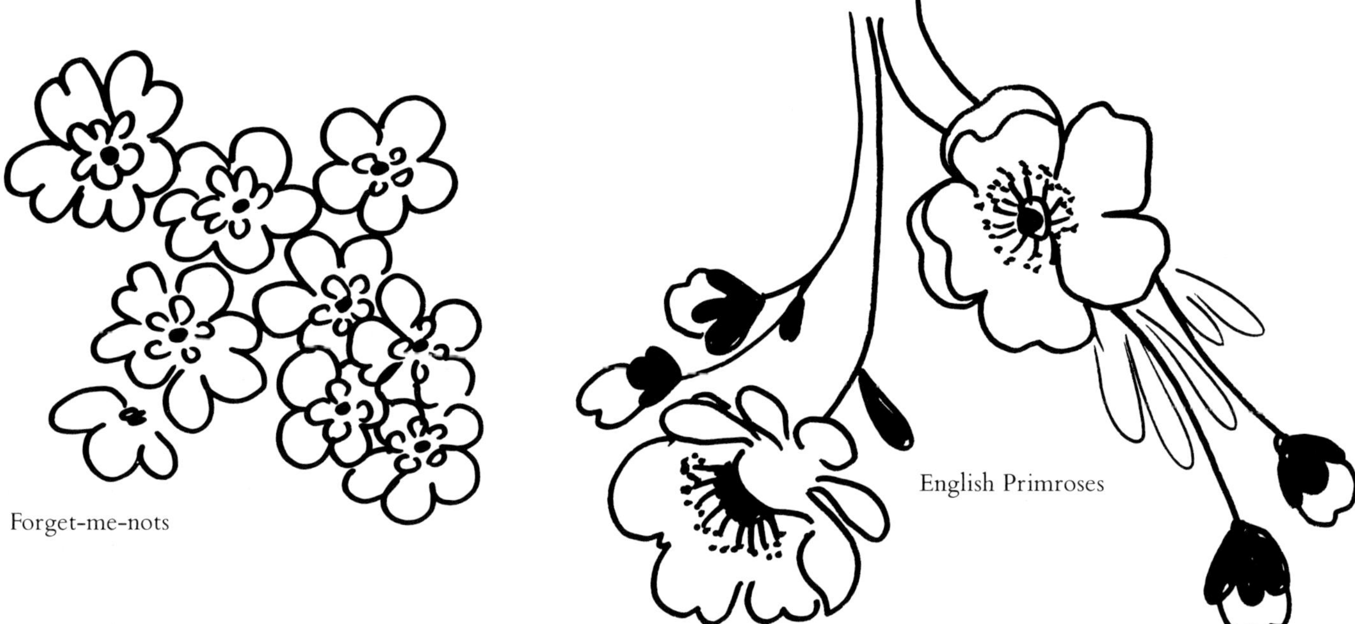

Forget-me-nots

English Primroses

j. Forget-me-not: Use a Raphael No. 3 brush
The dark side (right) has Ultramarine Blue petals.

The light side petals are painted in a mixture of Sapphire Blue and Warm White.

The inner petals around the centre are small comma strokes in Warm White.

The centre is a Yellow Light dot.

k. English Primroses: Use a Raphael No. 3 brush
The outer edge of the petals are painted in a mixture of Warm White and Yellow Oxide. They gradually darken towards the centre in Yellow Oxide.

The buds are painted in Yellow Oxide.

The centres of the flowers are painted in a mixture of Teal Green and Cadmium Yellow Mid, as are the leaves and calyxes.

Dot Cadmium Yellow Mid around the centres.

l. Tuberoses: Use a Raphael No. 3 brush
These tubular flowers are painted in a mixture of Moss Green and Warm White, with a sideload of Warm White. The centres of the flowers and the leaves are painted in Green Oxide with Cadmium Yellow highlight.

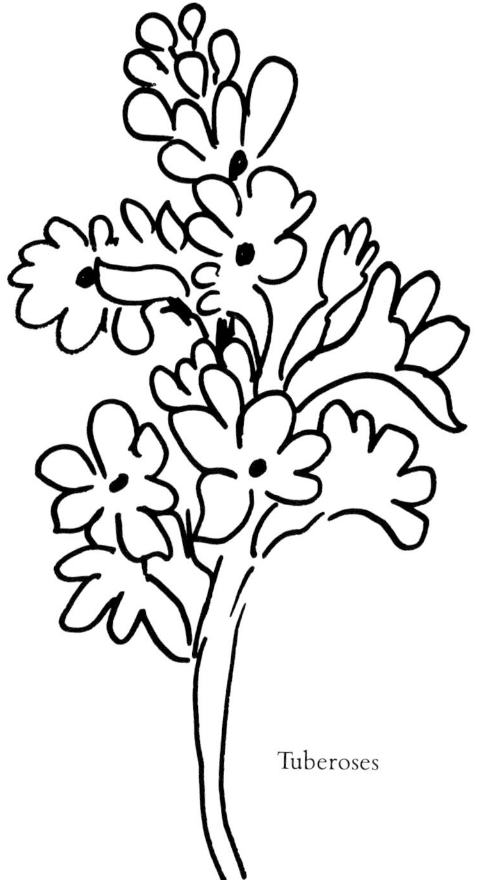

Tuberoses

m. Clusters of Small Roses: Use a Raphael No.3 brush The method is the same as the large centre rose.

Paint the roses in a mixture of Red Earth plus Fawn plus Warm White. Highlight with Warm White.

The centre stamens are Raw Sienna.

The leaves and calyxes are in Teal Green, while the veins are in Smoked Pearl.

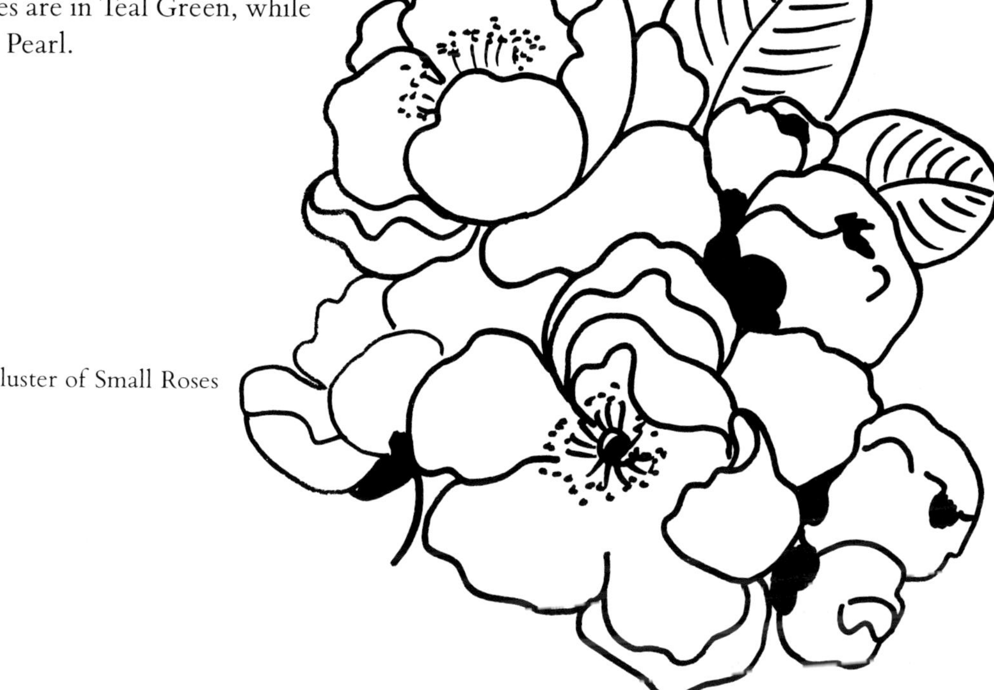

Cluster of Small Roses

■ FRAME:

First coat the frame in French Blue.

The second coat is a mixture of French Blue and Warm White.

Using Wet and Dry Sandpaper plus warm water, sand the frame until it has a desired affect. Always wipe the excess paint off with a paper towel while sanding to see how much paint has been removed.

The inner frame around the vase of flowers is painted in Warm White.

■ Antique.

■ Varnish.

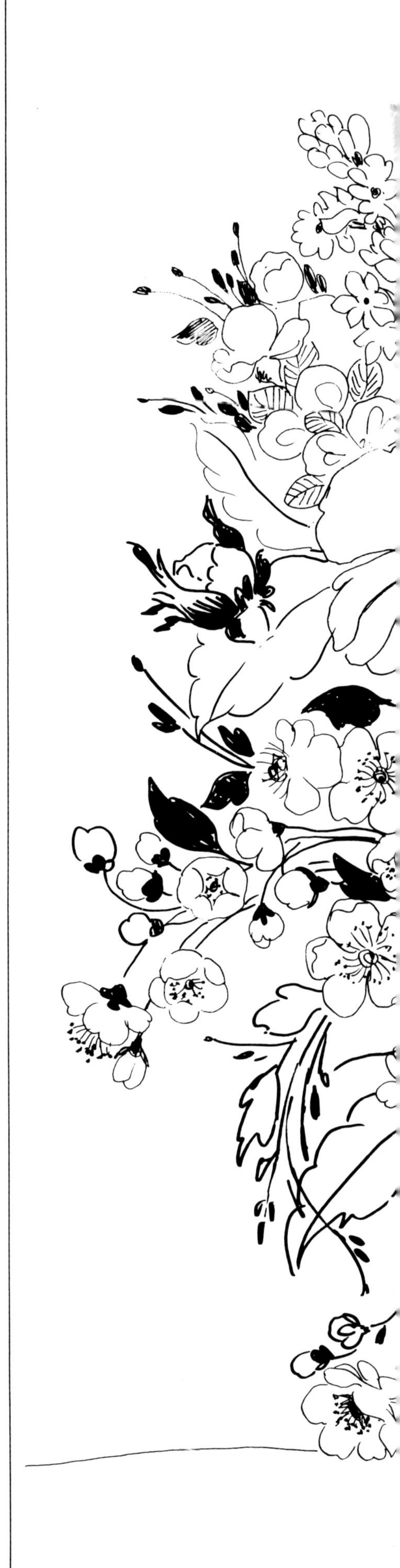

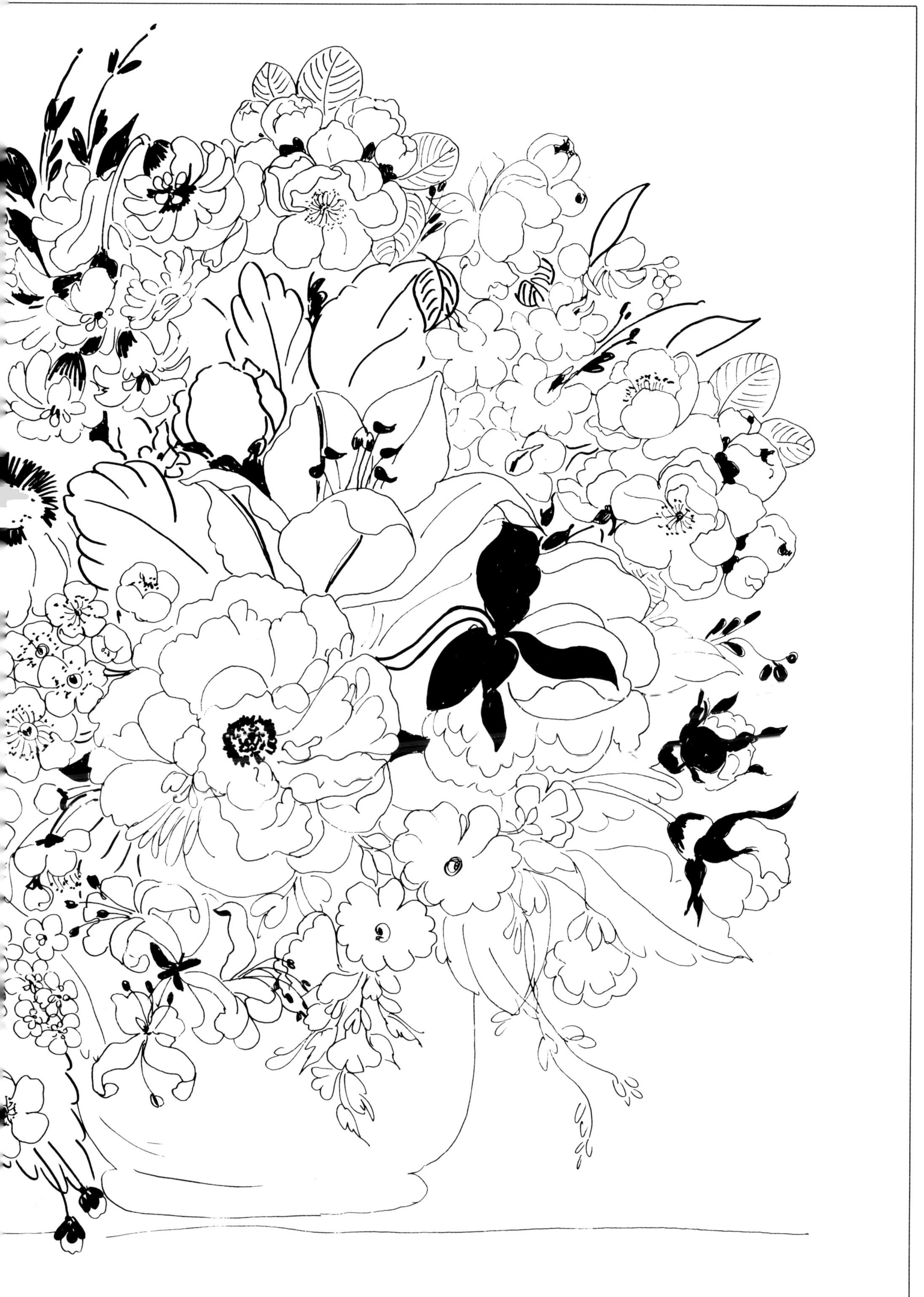